SURFACING SADNESS

A Centennial of Korean-American Literature 1903-2003

SURFACING SADNESS

A Centennial of
Korean-American Literature
1903-2003

Edited by

Yearn Hong Choi, Ph.D.
Haeng Ja Kim

HOMA & SEKEY BOOKS
DUMONT, NEW JERSEY

First American Edition
Copyright © 2003 by Homa & Sekey Books

All rights reserved. No part of this book may be reproduced, stored in a retrieval system, or transmitted in any form, or by any means, electronic, mechanical, photocopying, recording or otherwise, without prior permission from the publisher.

Library of Congress Cataloging-in-Publication Data

Ch'oe, Yæon-hong (Choi, Yearn Hong), 1941-
Surfacing sadness: a centennial of korean-american literature 1903-2003 / Yearn Hong Choi & Haeng Ja Kim.—1st ed.
p. cm.
ISBN 1-931907-09-9 (Hardcover)
1. American literature—Korean American authors. 2. Korean Americans—Literary collections. 3. Korean American literature—United States. 4. Korean American literature—United States—History and criticism. I. Kim, Haeng-ja, 1948-II. Title.
PS508.K67C46 2003
810.8'08957—dc21
2003003744

Published by Homa & Sekey Books
103-138 Veterans Plaza
Dumont, NJ 07628

Tel: (201)384-6692
Fax: (201)384-6055
Email: info@homabooks.com
Website: www.homabooks.com

Editor-in-chief: Shawn X. Ye
Executive editor: Judy Campbell

Printed in the United States of America
1 3 5 7 9 10 8 6 4 2

To all Korean-American poets and writers who have been crafting their art in their mother tongue

Table of Contents

Congratulatory Messages .... *xiii*
   Sung Chul Yang, Ph.D...*xv*
   Donald C. W. Kim ....*xvi*
   Yoon-Soo Park... *xviii*
Editorial Board..*xxi*
Introduction .... *xxiii*

POETRY 1

Nam Soo Park 3
   Seagull 3
   Name Analysis 4
   Autumn Embedded with Black Seed 5
   Guggenheim Museum 6
   Daytona Beach... 7
   Deer 8

Ko Won... 9
   Born Again in Dark Tears.. 9
   L. A. Elegy.. 13

Byong Hyon Kim 15
   Disapproving Reaction 15
   A Road Farthest from This Life 17

Yearn Hong Choi 19
   Black Korean 19
   Journeys to Korea 20
   Sound of Water 20
   For a Reunion 21
   The Woods.. 22
   March.. 23

Haeng Ja Kim **24**
   Like a Dandelion Seed 24
   February 26
   Flower of Ice 27
   Longing for the Homeland 28
   That Autumn 29
Yong Pal Kim **30**
   Im-jin River 30
   Echo 31
   At the Backyard 32
   Dusk 33
Yoon Ho Cho **34**
   A Dandelion 34
   The Two Faces of Love 35
Jung Ja Choi **36**
   Tulip 36
   Fallen Leaves 1 37
Sang Hee Kwak **38**
   To A Jewish Poet—for Yaffa Zins 38
   The Manhattan Sky-9.11 39
Ho Gill Kim **40**
   Meditation 40
   Cold Mountain 40
   Snow Talk 41
   Interrogation 41
   Niagara Falls 42
Hye Young Hahn **43**
   A Dry Cleaner Ironing the Pacific Ocean 43
   Two in the Afternoon Protest 44
Soon Tae Song **45**
   Transfer 45
   Winter Star 46
   Dust 47
   Television 48
   Photograph 49
Mee Soon Bae **50**
   Canvas 50
   Eulogy to Women 51
Yong Chin Chong **52**
   Holding up High the Torch of Korea's Spirit 52
Moon Hee Kim **55**
   Magnolia 55
   Grafting 56

TABLE OF CONTENTS

    May's Sunlight 57
William D. Chun 58
    An Alien's Elegance I 58
    An Alien's Elegance II 59
    However, Homeland Is in Spring Yet 60
Sunghee Cho 62
    Long Weekend 62
    Shadow Reading 63
Chungmi Kim 64
    Brother 64
    Returning 67
    Off to the Grammys 68
    I am 70
Chang Yun Lee 72
    Daily Bread 72
    Sky Above the Orchard 73
Samuel Changhyun Yim 74
    Father and Seal 74
    And the Day After 75
Hye Shin Lim 77
    Cold Medicine 77
    Worn Wooden Pier 79
    A Woman Worker Eating a Mango 80
Kwi Soon Kwon 81
    Apricot Blossom 81
    Evening Birds 82
    Sleep on the Fallen Leaves 83
Soon Paik 84
    Spring Rain 84
    Rain Drops 85
    Sound of Autumn 86
    Resurrection 87
    Annapolis 88
Ryang Suh 89
    Fried Locusts 89
    Bear Mountain Sonata 90
Young Kyo Kim 91
    Traffic Lights 91
    Music 92
Duk Jae Shin 94
    You, Go to Alaska to Get Aurora Down in Your Palm 94

ESSAYS 97

Dae Wook Chang 99
At a Grocery Store 99
Ke Hyang Lee 101
By the Window 101
Wan Soo Byun 105
The Return of the Prodigal Son............................. 105
Jay Sang Rhee 109
Father and Son 109

SHORT STORIES 113

Yong Ik Kim 115
The Wedding Shoes 115
Sang Ok Song 129
Echo 129
Young K. Hahn 137
Guest 137
Elsie Hyeryung Kim..163
The Swallow 163
Seulhee Ahn 170
A Tale from the Cornfield..................................... 170
Mia Yun 185
The Carp 185
Kyung Sook Park 193
The Caveman Who Left His Cave Country 193

CONCLUSION 209
Korean Literature in the United States: At the Centennial................ 209

CONGRATULATORY MESSAGES

CONGRATULATORY MESSAGES

Sung Chul Yang, Ph.D.
Korean Ambassador to the United States of America

ON JANUARY 13, 1903, one hundred and two people from Korea disembarked from the merchant ship *Gaelic* in Honolulu, Hawaii. They were the first group of Koreans to work on the sugar-cane plantation. From such humble beginnings, the Korean-American population has blossomed to number some two million people who are now making great strides in all aspects of American life.

Surfacing Sadness: A Centennial of Korean-American Literature is a timely publication which reviews and examines one-hundred years of Korean immigration to America. Since Younghill Kang's English literary work, *Poems of the Orient*, many Korean-American writers have emerged to leave their mark on American literature. "The Wedding Shoes" by Yong Ik Kim and *The Martyred* by Richard E. Kim have received wide, critical acclaim. Following in their footsteps, second- and third-generation Korean-American writers, such as Chang Rae Lee and Cathy Song are now introducing Korean literature to American society.

I believe that the publication of *Surfacing Sadness* provides a rare glimpse into the lives of Korean-Americans. This publication is to be commended for strengthening the bonds among Korean-Americans and for its contributing to the understanding of Korean culture and tradition in America.

Donald C. W. Kim
Chair, Centennial Committee of Korean Immigration to the United States of America, Center for Korean Studies, Honolulu, Hawaii

Aloha,

ON JANUARY 13, 1903, the first Korean immigrants stepped on the sands of Hawaii in search of a new life. Many others followed them in waves of immigration as Korean Americans have spread throughout the United States during the past one hundred years. Among the first Korean-American immigrants and in each generation since, Korean-American poets and writers have surfaced as contributors to a growing, unsung tradition of literary works. This community of writers has chronicled Korean-American dreams, hopes, despair, and pain. As the national celebration of the Centennial for Korean Immigration to the United States of America begins, the publication of *Surfacing Sadness* provides a long-awaited platform for the presentation, appreciation, and review of one hundred years of Korean-American literature.

On behalf of the Centennial Committee of Korean Immigration to the United States, it is my distinct pleasure to congratulate all writers, translators, editors, and members of the Korean Poets and Writers Association. I would also like to express my deep appreciation for the dedicated efforts that have resulted in this publication that links the generations of the Korean immigrant literary experience to mainstream American literature.

I am also grateful to the sponsorship of George Washington University and the Smithsonian Institution for support and interest in this project that contributes to the field of comparative study of Korean-American and Korean literary works around the world. As one of the co-sponsoring organizations, the Centennial Committee is proud to be part of this worthy project that is bringing the Korean-American experience to light in a way that every generation of Korean-Americans and mainstream American society can appreciate and enjoy for many years to come.

To the writers who went before to give literary life to a first generation of Korean immigrants in 1903, I offer my respect and admiration. To the up-and-coming generation of Korean-American writers, I express my sincere wish that your works will become widely known in mainstream American society as distinct contributions to world literary tradition and lauded as an excellent expression of individual talent.

With my heartfelt congratulations.

Yoon-Soo Park
President, the Centennial Committee of Korean Immigration to the United States-Greater Washington (CCKI-GW)

I AM HAPPY to see the publication of this commemorative book, *Surfacing Sadness*, the Korean-American centennial anthology. Intended to introduce the works of Korean-American writers to the American public, this much-anticipated work breaks new and important literary ground. I never realized how many gifted authors and poets of Korean heritage are creating such wonderful literary works in this hemisphere. This fine volume forever assuages such doubts.

While preparing for the Centennial Year of Korean Immigration in 2003, we found ample citation of the many achievements of Korean-Americans in politics, business, science, medicine, and sports in the United States. However, documentation of literary accomplishments of the first generation of Korean-Americans was unfortunately scarce.

It is my earnest hope that this collection of literary works will bring much-needed exposure to the Korean spirit, emotions, and ideals, and encourage the American public to appreciate the traditional, and unique, aspects of Korean culture.

There is a Chinese proverb that says, "Dim ink is better than a strong memory." This book eloquently illustrates the hope and desperation, the happiness and the heartache, of the Korean immi-

CONGRATULATORY MESSAGES

grants of the past hundred years who crossed the Pacific Ocean to achieve their dreams in the New World. I hope it will also inspire youth of all backgrounds who have literary aspirations to follow in the footsteps of these writers.

We, the Centennial Committee, are proud to present this work as a very important part of the Centennial celebration.

EDITORIAL BOARD

Co-Editors
Yearn Hong Choi
Haeng Ja Kim

Managing Editor
Stephen Henkin

Editorial Board
Wan Soo Byun
Yearn Hong Choi
Hyo-goo Jeong
Haeng Ja Kim
Won Ko
Kae-Woong Myung
Sang Ok Song
Dong Ha Yi

INTRODUCTION

THIS BOOK IS dedicated to the Korean-American poets and writers who have been crafting their art in their mother tongue in order to celebrate the centennial year of the first Koreans landing in Hawaii. The historic, maiden voyage of immigrants left Korea in December 1902 and arrived in Honolulu on January 13, 1903. The arrival in Hawaii of seven-thousand Koreans between 1903 and 1905 was the first wave of Korean immigrants to the United States. Then, the Japanese colonial ruler stopped the immigration, even though Hawaii's sugar plantations greatly needed the Korean workers.

January 13, 2003 will mark the Centennial commemoration of the embarking of the American merchant ship *Gaelic*, from the Korean port of Jae-Mul, across the Pacific Ocean to the first steps of the 102 Koreans at the port of Honolulu. To realize their dreams, they began their lives of hard labor on the sugarcane plantations. Dispersed with blood and sweat through many vicissitudes, the first page of the immigrant history began. Even in dire conditions, the immigrant pioneers accumulated funds for their nation and for regaining its independence. They promoted the foundation of the national independence of the motherland, which had lost its sovereignty. After overcoming such adversities, the Korean-American society produced judges, lawyers, professors, doctors, engineers, journalists, executives, and other professionals for mainstream America, thus, developing into a proud ethnic group.

Today, to commemorate this progress, contemporary Korean-American scholars have launched a series of scholarly and historical conferences to review the first hundred years of Korean life in the United States. They especially look forward to seeing a more vital connection to their cultural roots. Thus, this book represents Korean-American poets and writers in the Korean language whose works have been translated into English. This book will contrast with another volume to be published by the University of Hawaii Press, with noted Korean novelists Younghill Kang, Richard Kim, and Chang Rae Lee who have produced their works in English.

The Korean-American poets and writers contributing here cannot distance themselves from their beloved mother tongue, or the culture that has so deftly shaped the approach to their craft. These poets and writers living in America have been writing continuously and tirelessly in the Korean language, but they have by and large been overlooked, both in the United States and in their homeland.

In the literary field, Younghill Kang (1899-1972) was the first Korean-American to publish his work in English. His first collection, *Poems of the Orient*, was published in 1929. Kang, an English literature graduate of Harvard University, focused his work on novels. His first autobiographical work, *The Grass Roof*, received critical acclaim, earning the Book of the Century award. Later, Yong Ik Kim, a first-generation author, published his short story, "The Wedding Shoes," in the June 1956 issue of *Harper's Bazaar*, thus emerging into the American literary world with praise.

Surfacing Sadness will be the first serious effort in encompassing Korean-American works in mass by the authors of different genres. Furthermore, this collection of literary works will play a significant role in not only handing down an important cultural inheritance and the spirit of the Korean immigrants to future generations, but also by bringing together two million Korean-Americans, enclosing generation gaps into one ethnic group.

Literature requires the perfect command of language. Unfortunately, these dedicated Korean immigrants have not acquired the

INTRODUCTION

language skill to write their works in English. Despite neglect and embarrassment, there must be jewels in the mud. That is the spirit of this book. Even though our dauntless writers' imperfect English and strong accents have been hampering their entry into mainstream America, their ideas and literary quality should not be neglected. This book is a Korean scream in the castle. Anyway, literature is the work of the outcast. Is it not?

In April 1996, Yearn Hong Choi read his poems in the United States Library of Congress under the auspices of the Gertrude Clarke Whitthall Poetry and Literature Fund. He recited them in his mother tongue, and even though the American audience could not understand his language, they still listened intently. The listeners were inspired by the passion inherent in the Korean language. Such elevated passion is common for the writers contained herein. Except for a couple of poets and one writer in this book, the great majority of the contributors have never had their poems, essays, and short stories published in American literary magazines. Since the works in this book are translations from the Korean language, needless to say, the original meanings and cadences may be somewhat lost in the process of translation. But that is an acceptable trade in exchange for the raw emotion and range of experience that emerges.

Of course, this volume will contrast with the University of Hawaii publication. Certainly there are two rivers flowing. We hope they meet somewhere in the vast waters between our two homes. Poets and writers for this book were selected by Yearn Hong Choi, Hyogoo Jeong, and Won Ko (poetry), Dong-ha Yi and Sang-ok Song (short story), and Wan Soo Byun and Kae-Woong Myung (essay). The final selection of the contributed works was done by Stephen Henkin, arts editor of *The World & I* magazine. The kind assistance of the above people is greatly appreciated.

We also like to express our gratitude to Donald CW Kim, general chairman of the Centennial committee of Korean Immigration to the US and Yoon Soo Park, chairman of the CCKI-

Greater Washington who provided generous funding for this volume.

Yearn Hong Choi
Haeng Ja Kim
Co-Editors

POETRY

Nam Soo Park

Seagull

They do not live here
Not because they like the sea.
They do not live here
Not because they like the memories of the sea.
Seagulls are birds that
Thrive from the sea.
Just living off the sea.
Gliding and diving over the water's waves,
Ignited by the turbulent storms
That could rock a 100,000-ton vessel,
Seagulls are born here,
Live here, and die here.
Seagull is not a bird.
It itself is the sea.
It is the sea.

Name Analysis

1

I am often asked,
What is your name?
When told, P.A.R.K.
Park, Common response is
Are you Tong Sun Park's relative
Or are you related to President Park?
Startling me.

When tired of name analysis,
one gentleman asks,
Is your store supported by the Unification Church's money?
Complaining preposterously.

2

A large black man suddenly greets me,
—"Ahn Nyung Ha Sip Ni Ca?"
He is a Korean War veteran.

He calls out an unrecognizable women's name
Repeating "Paju Paju"
But a name that ends with "Ja" is not a few.

With a heart full of
The desire to weep,
It is an evening of remembering the motherland.

Autumn Embedded with Black Seed

When the autumn embedded with black seeds
Is sorted into a bag,
The year is almost gone.

It is the autumn legs feeling chill
When cool wind blows away.
The seed bag is exposed to fresh air.

Clear sunlight burns
On a folded, expanding sky
Now it would be all right for the farmer to rest.

Guggenheim Museum

When I take the spiral steps,
I meet the most beautiful colors
Of this world.
In a corner of New York City's darkened heart,
An incomprehensive space spreads out.
In front of it,
People cleansed their dimmed eyes.
Picasso's painting sided by Gauguin's sunny Tahiti,
Degas' nice-looking, young ladies dance.
One day time, never bored
I take the spiral steps. Again,
I look down the most beautiful space
Of this world
From early March.

Daytona Beach

There is no winter
At Daytona Beach
Even in winter.
It is in the sunshine
White
After discoloring all colors.
Parts of naked bodies in the sunshine
Are covered by a size of leaf.
Without shame or guilt
They embrace each other and roll over.
Red yacht over the distant horizon
is passing by.
The yacht is smaller than a woman's pant.

Deer

There is one dead deer
On the 46th highway.
There are still tears
In his eyes.
It was a mistake
To judge:
There would be no gunpoint aimed at him in the darkness.
No, he was embarrassed by the bright headlight.
Death came so suddenly.

TRANSLATED BY YEARN HONG CHOI

Nam Soo Park, now deceased, wrote 324 poems during his life. His first poetry book, *Lantern*, was published in 1940, and his last book, *Narrow Road*, came out in 1994. All of Park's poems can be considered as imagist, and his last twenty-four years in the United States told of the painful life of an immigrant.

Ko Won

Born Again in Dark Tears

I

The woman was tottering.
She was scared by her own legs.
The very moment her sight was blurred
suddenly, dizzily,
something black—with a flash—
was caught in her hand.
The hand turned black right away.

The whole world,
indeed the whole wide world
only looked black.
The woman's mind was also
becoming charcoal, pitch-black.
She heard in her heart
coals tumbling.

The woman was tempted
to blacken a black color
with a black color
just to make it
blacker and blacker.
She wanted thereby
herself to burn black, burn black.

II

A woman was taking aim
at a woman's life
filled with grief.

She was at once aiming at every
Korean woman's all sorts of grief.

Exactly aiming at
the way of life called immigration,
the name immigration,
double nationalities of Korea and the U.S.,
the language itself that had been lost
somewhere, nowhere, now that
she spoke neither Korean nor English,
and her own resentment
cursing Heaven for this and for that,
all the many black colors,
she was merely taking aim at them
with herself being in black, black.

A second and another second
passing in a flash,
an instant she was aiming
at a thing that is nothing,
vanity of vanities,
and at an empty air,
the woman was on fire herself.

III

"Eli, Eli,
lama sabachthani?"
A .38 caliber handgun.
Who played the fool?
To nobody's knowledge, Good
Heavens, in less than a second,
a bullet dashed out.
It dared to shoot through
somebody in front.

Having held a gun, the woman acting
against the ten commandments after all,
against her own prayer,
the hand killed Latasha—
a fifteen-year-old black girl.
The hand, now burning black,
had to tear the woman's heart.

The woman wanted to see her blood.
She only wanted to let a sea
of black blood run on from her.
Eli, Eli, the woman
wanted to fall down herself also
and to shed only black blood
with no end,
with no cross visible.

IV

"Oh, no,
not this, please,
no probation.
It's ridiculous to keep me,
the criminal, alive and to cause
all the Blacks
and Koreans to die."

"I must go, I must go.
A sinner who had chosen to come
to a place she was not supposed to be in
certainly must go with no-one's pardon."

"But what,
what is all this in the world?
What's happening to my life?"

V

It was wrong.
Everything was wrong.
And yet someday, the woman from Seoul
was being born again.

Mrs. "Two" on her way to rebirth
had to stand on a new hill of soul
where two turns to one:
neither a Black nor a Korean,
now one Korean-Black.
A woman to be born again
in the beautiful black color,
a color even prettier
than that of a Korean child
born of a Black father.

A descendant of the black bear,
a woman with black hair, a black skirt,
doomed to be born again
as a Korean-Black,
she is crying, wishing not to be
but to be born again.
Her soul cries, praying, in dark tears,
in dark tears.

(Published in *American Journal,* 19-2, 1993)

[Note] "Two" in section V is coined from the Korean woman's last name, Tu.

L. A. Elegy

In the strange evening of the day
when a streak of the devil-dark news
strangled Los Angeles,
the city of a false name
has suddenly fallen into hell,
no later than the sun sunk into the Pacific.
Land and sky turning to a sea of fire,
flame-columns thrusting through
smoke-clouds,

L.A. in late April is caught in
rioting fires.

Black is buried in blazes,
white and yellow and green
all mixed are jet-black and glaring red.
Tough iron gates popping up hard,
the angels' rainbow broken down,
all colors are on fire.

What else, what more
is really, really burning?
Hatred, mistrust, murder,
discrimination, frustration,
wrath, and despair:
are all these what's being burned?
Both goodness and evil,
because of its own good and evil,
are all on fire, endless fire?

It's still far from an end.
Many more, much more
of misunderstanding and swindling
should burn more.

SURFACING SADNESS

Burn black.
Burn red.
A deep-hidden conflagration,
the great combustion
L.A. has long waited for
should burn all the more.

Oh yes,
more of tears, bloody tears,
the history of tears as well,
burn all now
and burn altogether,
altogether.

(1992)

Ko Won is a winner of the Kansas City Star Award for poetry, a member of P.E.N. Center, USA, and of the American Literary Translators Association. Ko is publisher and editor of *Munhak Segye/The Literary Realm* and director of the Kulmaru Institute of Literature in Los Angeles, and has published a number of poetry books, including *The Turn of Zero, Some Other Time, Contemporary Korean Poetry, South Korean Poets of Resistance, Voices in Diversity,* and *Buddhist Elements in Dada: A Comparison of Tristan Tzara, Takahashi Shinkichi, and Their Fellow Poets.*

Byong Hyon Kim

Disapproving Reaction

In the immigrated country, *kimchi* and soy paste
Has to be eaten in stealth.

Like a thieving cat, we have to eat *kimchi* and soy paste in hiding
Using this country's toothpaste and mouth wash and gum and soap and perfume
In abundance and pretending like they weren't eaten
The neighbor's nose, like that of the dog, gives the expression of disapproving reaction.

The foolish thieving cat, believing all the television ads of this country's
Toothpaste and mouth wash and gum and soap and perfume and pretend
Like he didn't eat *kimchi* and soy paste and play a hand at love, but,
The heart of this country's women, like that of the dog, cannot be fooled and he gets
Disapproving reaction.

The foolish, thieving cat avoids *kimchi* and soy paste as much as possible and avoids,
Conversations, laughs, cries, opening of the mouth, as much as possible and do the
Yawning, burping, and breathing out in hiding and even after washing every nook of the
Body like a monastic monk with a good soap, the smell hidden so well that
This country's expression of disapproving reaction is lodged solidly like a stone.

SURFACING SADNESS

The foolish thieving cat, doesn't seem to know that the smell of
   kimchi and soy
Paste is arising from our blood and soul and the smell would be
   there even if
We don't eat *kimchi* and soy paste.

A Road Farthest from This Life

A road farthest from this life is the other side of the earth.
If not, could it be the distance to that yonder star?
For the lifers of prison, the threshold of the jail, for a man with a crush,
The loved one's heart, for the separated families,
The demilitarized zone is the farthest from this life.

For the half way around the earth or to the star, high tech can be used,
The lifers can be released on good behavior,
the man with a crush could deliver a bundle
of pure love daily; erasing the farthest distance from this life
would need less than a piece of rubber eraser.

The separated families, during the separated fifty years, have mastered
The Sa-Myung-Dang's method of contracting earth's space, combined
The body and mind and prayer into a marathoner's feet, and ran and ran
In their dreams, but, even now the division is still running in its place.
The distance of the demilitarized zone is the farthest from this life.

On my Guinness book, the immigrants who aged and died
Unable to go back to the homeland, therefore, even after death,
Unable to close their eyes, buried in a foreign land, the time
These people would have their eyes closed, is recorded as the
Farthest from this life.

TRANSLATED BY EUNHWA CHOE

SURFACING SADNESS

Byong Hyon Kim, former president of the Korean Literary Society in Los Angeles, is a recipient of the Life-Time Achievement Award in Poetry.

Yearn Hong Choi

Black Korean

The Korean man moved to a Hawaiian sugar plantation
at the turn of the century,
and to Mexico's henequen fields,
and finally moved to Cuba's sugar plantation
to make a few dollars.

His grandson, I met in the District of Columbia,
only knew that his grandpa was a Korean man,
but did not know why he was in Cuba.
The old man was supposedly in the Hermit Kingdom.

The Korean man fell in love with a black woman in Cuba,
and had a son, who moved to Miami as a refugee,
and then moved to the District of Columbia.

Jose Suh, I know, has an odd last name.
The Chosun's seed was not just planted in Cuba.
It was also planted in Central Asia desert,
and cold wind of Sakhalin as well.

I see a Korean man's anger, frustration, love, and
affection in the black of his grandson.
I see the demise of the Chosun Kingdom in
a Black-Korean American from Cuba,
and the Korean odyssey.

Journeys to Korea

Even though only an empty house
awaits me, I go.
I beg pardon of my ancestors,
buried in my family cemetery
up in the mountains.
I beg forgiveness; a son living abroad
so long in a foreign land.

Sound of Water

It is not
Magpies nor winds passing the pines.
It is the sound of mountain shadow
Moving toward the village.
It is the sound of silently
Flying creatures and the fish underneath
The rocks.
It is the sound of a poet's footsteps
Never visited.
It is the sound of cleanliness,
Freshness of summer.
Light as the feather of a mountain bird.
The poor villagers were listening
To the midsummer night's sound of water,
and were falling asleep.

For a Reunion

30 years have passed away
without our notice.
Once we shake hands with each other
In the corner,
The years are equated by the moment
After our hug.
Our past and yearning for each other become more
Beautiful flowers in our heart.
Past tense of young and relentless wandering, love and pain
In this new land is replaced by
The present tense
Of rare purity.
"How could I forget you?"
You have been in my safe all the years.
A few more drinks offer joy and ease;
Life is short and art is long,
Then long years could be shorter.
"Don't feel bad!"
We are still young,
Years come to our memory
Like a port I visited in the south sea.
…All that glitters is not gold
All that glitters is our growth
And yearning in long distance.

The Woods

The woods
are composed of trees.
Trees are free in
finding their places
and their height,
but they are neat in the woods.
Squirrels, fruits, beasts, wells,
berries, morning glory, and dew
and diamonds are
in the woods.
Waterfalls.
river under the rocks,
Nymph's shower,
and her clothes
(not stolen by a woodcutter)
are all beautiful.
The woods belong to the trees.
The woods belong to the saint.
The saint is hiding all the
beautiful things with the green
leaves from modern man
who is passing by
the woods
65 mph.

March

Forsythia has already become forsythia.
The soapy smell of a woman's hair
Is refreshing.
Now it has begun to confuse.
Clear winter night sky's stars
No longer clear like the rising heat waves.
Yes. Warm things equal confusion.
Forsythia hides chicks.
Seduction seeps into a woman.
Water is rising in the trees.
The world is experiencing heated confusion.
Men break the flowered boughs
While whistling.

Yearn Hong Choi, founding president of the Korean Poets and Writers Group in the Washington, D.C. area, has published his poems in the P.*E.N. International, Poetry USA*, the *Washington Post*, *Wyoming, Mildred, disOrient* and *The World & I*; his review essays in *World Literature Today*; and short stories in *Short Story International* and *Intercultural Journeys Through Reading and Writing* (New York: HarperCollins, 1991), among others. Choi's poems have been translated into Portuguese and published in Brazil. His literary essays have appeared in the *Washington Post, Los Angeles Times, Japan Times, Korea Herald* and the *Korea Times*, for which he is currently a columnist.

Haeng Ja Kim

Like a Dandelion Seed
—100th Anniversary of Korean-American Immigration

When our lives were young like those trees
with a goal to live better, came half way around the globe,
we carried a handful of earth from our country
and lowered our sail
on the giant continent of America.
With two fists and an able body as possessions,
we tearfully left our motherland
only with a "can do" will and a lonely fight ahead.
The tight hold on my skirt hem
and the little ones' petrified cries
pulled off every dawn,
turned away with tightened throats, our young days
resurrecting in delicate pain.

We weren't the only ones with pain.
Through the closed eyes, Port Jaemulpo can be seen.
In that winter with the family aboard the American ship,
Gaelic, with the white robes fluttering in the wind,
the tears shed on the deck by the Chosun people, the tears
which wet the Pacific Ocean.
In retrospect, on the long-ago Hawaiian sugar-cane plantations,
with the back-breaking labor,
the sweat and blood money was saved and sent
as the Independence funds, our ancestors
adhering spirit of patriotism can be seen.

Sowing the dream in the barren foreign land
on the Atlantic, or perhaps the Pacific coast
like a dandelion seed landing anywhere
they lived well making the nests.

Now and then when we glance toward the east,
my heart would become numb.
With longing, looking up at the dawn sky,
a tap on my shoulder in reassurance
was the dark indigo waters of the East Sea.

Now let us all stand
and erect the five-thousand years
worth of spirit and culture on this land
As the light of the coarse sea of life,
light the million immigrants path.
Here
this huge American continent
this is the land we will need to love forever and ever.

We shall become a handful of compost, only by decaying.

TRANSLATED BY EUNHWA CHOE

February

Between snowstorm and crocus bloom
there is a road to a maiden's cottage
no one sees.
Between January and March
there is a secret love, its heat
breaking through the frozen winter land.

When a new dawn falls on the steps
of morning dew, a young man marries
a young woman.
Although the new bride spent all winter
in solitude
her breasts have swollen.

Like ice flowers on the deadly tree branches,
the coming birth is anticipated, a flowered blanket
spread next to the fireplace.
Can you hear the sound?
Water is flowing through
all the veins of the tree.

Please touch me,
a new baby in my womb
is kicking me, so strong.
Oh, I am thrilled by this sign of life.
Please put your ear to my womb.

TRANSLATED BY YEARN HONG CHOI

Flower of Ice

You are
my dream
and will.

You are
my hope
and despair.

You are
my prayer
and yearning.

Oh, you are
my flower of ice.

TRANSLATED BY YEARN HONG CHOI

Longing for the Homeland

Now I know,
Why, when the first flower bud at the foot of Mount Halla bursts into a blossom,
All blossoms of the spring face the North.

Over the truce iron railings,
From far away Northern land,
The Mount Paikdoo lake rushes the thunder clouds
Taking all the rivers to the sky.
After enveloping all the nooks of the Provinces of Chosun,
Why, it buries itself in our hearts
Now, I know

The ownerless helmet a the Demilitarized Zone
A heap of wild grasses,
Guarding it alone.
Every autumn, it floats bruised longings
Toward only to the South, to the South.

Now I know,
Why, a snowy night of the quiet and forlorn mountains,
The nightly soft cry of the Imjin River,
Crying and weeping, rising to the top, settling down on my shoulders.

TRANSLATED BY EUNHWA CHOE

That Autumn

That Autumn in my twenties
lives within my heart

After getting out of long working hours
I closed the curtain.
Through the window, I glanced at the dusk
Across the forest.

The wind across the empty field
reaches the forest
Like a faint whistle.

Sometimes,
bitter-sweet fragrances of wild flowers
comforted my tired mind,
That autumn in my twenties kindles fire
In the barren heart of my forties.

TRANSLATED BY EUNHWA CHOE

Haeng Ja Kim, former president of the Korean Poets and Writers Association in the Washington, D.C. area, has won poetry awards from the *Joong-Ang Daily* New Spring Literary Contest (Children's Poem, 1968) and the *Los Angeles' Korea Times* (1993). She is a recipient of the Editor's Choice Award from the National Library of Poetry in Maryland. Kim published *When I Close My Eyes, You Are*, a collection of poems, in 1995.

Yong Pal Kim

Im-jin River

The river is flowing.
It never ceases to move
But the bank is familiar.

Some flower petals are floating.
They all look busy riding their own wave.
But the woman on the bank is standing still.

Her man was gone
In the civil war.
But she is still roaming
Around his graveyard.

On this de-militarized zone
Where the touch-and-go specter
Is roaming,
Even birds cannot alight at ease.

Only the drizzle is whispering.
It should be Heaven's grace
Touching strings of the Earth.

The river is flowing.
It flows also in the woman's heart.
And, far afar, a monkey howls.

Echo

Somewhere in between heaven and earth,
There is a soul, my protector.

It always reveals a quiet love,
Echoing an invisible wink
At every incident.

It is neither a look nor a sound.
It is just an apocalypse.

Hoping the very moment to come
When I may cry up with awakening,

Wishing to scream like a crane
Toward the echo at a clear sky,

I am destined to climb everyday
This Steepy Mountain road.

At the Backyard

In my backyard,
I stretch a green-white parasol
Covering the white table.

Rose coquets in crimson,
Lawn is faithful with its deep green,
Soaking into my eyes freshly.

The table boasts with its accurate round,
The parasol is elaborate octagon,
Drawing my attention vividly.

Abrupt sound on my eardrum!
It is the grasshoppers' Te De'um!
Untimely but showery.

Casually I find
A rose-petal is falling.
Somebody has just passed by.

At the window of my study,
Little Lisa is beckoning,
"Grandpa! Hi!"

I raise my hand
Like a man in the train
And gesticulate "Goodbye!"

When I devoured everything around,
The water-tap was twinkling
Like a flashing tear in my eye.

Dusk

The snowfield was desolate,
Like a void in my heart.

And it was dyed orange
By the gorgeous evening glow.

It used to be His generous greeting
To His beloved Earth
At the end of every day.

This intimate twilight,
Passing by my whiskers,
Sighed, "It's night now!"

I tried to converse with Him
Only to feel discarded.
I had to go to bed like a dummy.

But, at last, I found myself listening
To the whispering of water vain
Flowing under the frozen earth.

Yong Pal Kim is a winner of the Golden Poet Award from World of Poetry, the Poetry Award from the Korean Literary Society of America, and the Outstanding Achievement in Poetry Award from the National Library of Poetry, in Maryland. Kim's four books of poetry are: *Ruins, A Toad's Talk, Pulses of Time*, and *Mr. Melange's Camera*. Kim also published a book of prose, *Stroll in the Wood of Lebanon*.

Yoon Ho Cho

A Dandelion
—Written in reflection on a racially motivated hate-crime that occurred in Indiana, on July 4, 1999

A white child
Picked a yellow dandelion.

Although it is a wild flower,
It is nevertheless beautiful.
And though it appears scentless,
It exudes a sweet, pleasant fragrance.
At seeing the flower, the boy rejoiced.

It harbored no expectation never to be picked,
Because it did not desire a happiness devoid of sorrow,
Nor ever a blue sky without a single cloud,
The dandelion simply sighed once and smiled.

White dandelion seeds,
After they have flown upon the autumn sky,
Come back into bloom every spring,
Yellow petals here and there,
To be remembered forevermore.

TRANSLATED BY KEEHWA HONG

POETRY

The Two Faces of Love

After you have lived for a while,
you find that everyday old things are pushed out
by new things into a garage sale.

Kitchen equipment,
old clothes,
old toys the children played with,
all these things we display for sale on a shelf.

We even sell the imperfect love
that we've become attached to over time.

A woman shouts,
"Selling my husband for a dollar.
Because I'm sick of him!"

After her love was sold cheaply,
after night comes and night has passed,
the woman shouts with tears in her eyes,
"Buying back my husband for 100 dollars.
I can't live without him!"

TRANSLATED BY RACHEL RHEE

Yoon Ho Cho is a winner of the New Writer Award from *Jayu Munhak* literature magazine and the Andes Literature Award. His publications include *Wanting to Meet the Wild Flowers* (1986), *The Poet's Tree* (1992), and *You, the Suffering Brooder* (1998). Cho currently compiles and edits the *Korean Expatriate Literature* magazine.

Jung Ja Choi

Tulip

From the edge of
the long corridor
comes the whispering of a futile rumor;

Locking them
inside a room
would be a vain effort;

The words
might sneak out;
The love, though, cannot be hidden.

Fallen Leaves 1

If heaven calls me today
I will go.

Is any life
in this world
not terminal?

Watching you fall to the ground
like chilly raindrops

I am helpless.

Those who are courageous
are swept by the wind;

those who are not
are dangling at the tip of branches,

hanging to this life,
footsteps of agony.

Dear wind,
give
me
the courage
to fall.

TRANSLATED BY JIN YOUNG PARK

Jung Ja Choi, former president of the Korean Writers Association in New York, has published seven volumes of poetry, including *Love for Daisy Fleabane Flowers* and *Returning Life*. She received the Chon Sang-byung literary prize from Seoul in 2002.

Sang Hee Kwak

To A Jewish Poet—for Yaffa Zins

In Autumn 1988 on Staten Island Ferry
Poetry Festival, we met.
At first sight, I felt your soul's pain,
your hope of returning to your roots.
The fall moon's yellow rays
floating over the waves of Hudson River,
like the gas of the death camps.

In your trembling gray eyes,
I saw your parents dying
in front of you.

Pain becomes endurable
only when there is hope.
Oh, my dear friend,
where are you now?
Are you still walking at dusk
in the streets of Jerusalem,

the sweet, spring breeze
on your cheek, soothing the hope
of peace, yours and mine?
Where are you now, my dear?

The Manhattan Sky-9.11

Today
like a wandering star i walk
feeling lost
fallen leaves on my feet, dry and scattered
The star hid at the daylight
Oh, the beauty of handshake
longing, missing you
damp with tears, yearning for you
I sought after the shadow of a bird
passing at the sky over empty
Manhattan

Today, What should i do?
Where do i go?
A wondering star
seeking tiny pieces of you gone
Traces of shattered dreams gone

But...
the green leaf
shoots anew
under the Manhattan sky,
as wandering star walking and hoping
fallen leaves on my feet.

Sang Hee Kwak has published five poetry books, two essays, and one novel. A recipient of the Olympoetry award from Spain and the Appreciation for Excellence in Poetry award, Kwak is currently conducting an English and Korean writing clinic in New York City.

Ho Gill Kim

Meditation

On the tip of a pine tree
a marsh tit is taking a sun bath.

With its bill buried in the feather, the bird
is completely free from all the worries.

Having a sun bath near the window myself,
I hardly notice my eyes being closed.

Cold Mountain

The moonlight sweeps the snowfield
and I watch the silvery mountain.
You ruminate inside, staying calm,
ten-thousand-year-old silence;
I cast my warm glance
on that cold quietude.

Snow Talk

Sitting out by the window together,
we are holding a cup of hot tea.

Simply mindless, facing each other,
you and I just exchange a smile.

Out there, snowflakes are piled up
On fir tree branches this deep night.

Interrogation

Lord, the Creator of the universe,
may I humbly ask you a question?
way out, ten billion light-years away,
that far, are you presently, all alone,
having fun with setting off fireworks
as you produce new stars and destroy them?

SURFACING SADNESS

Niagara Falls

Even beyond the heavenly kingdom,
there may be plenty of sad stories.
The Rocky Mountains in the far north
kept sending down snow and rain
til those tears became a long river;
now they roll over a sheer precipice.

TRANSLATED BY KO WON

Ho Gill Kim is editor of the quarterly literary magazine, *Sijo World*, and founder of the literary web sites, koreanwriters.com and sijoworld.com. Kim has published many poetry books, including *Sky Fantasia, Crystal Thirst,* and *Flower of Climax*. He has also been a Korean Airlines pilot, a columnist at the *Korean Central Daily News*, in Los Angeles, and president of Sunflower Farms.

Hye Young Hahn

A Dry Cleaner Ironing the Pacific Ocean

My younger brother abandoned his civil-servant position in Korea and migrated over the Pacific Ocean to New York. After becoming a dry-cleaner owner, he has been struggling with the wrinkles of the Pacific Ocean throughout the year; Pressed and pressed, it wouldn't smooth the Pacific Ocean, that indigo length of the skirt rushed in by fold upon fold of water bends; like some cheap, powdered detergent, the unsatisfying English language wouldn't bubble up well.

Should I sack it and go back?
I know how you feel.

I say I know but I can't even hold a seam of a skirt for him. Frankly, I am wearing the same messily wrinkled ocean for the past ten years, undulating in madness. In any case, if unable to tightly hold from this end to the other, dear brother, the ocean has to flutter in its wrinkles. Let it flutter. It is fortunate that there is an ocean that would stick to the thoroughly heated iron.

Isn't that so? Isn't that so?

With these words, the wave will rush in, in not so distant future, you will hear it in its entirety.

Two in the Afternoon Protest

Crawling into a phone receiver like an ant,
a glimpse, I peek in on the other side of the earth. Over there it's
three in the morning. Everyone would be asleep, grinding his
    teeth.
With a sleep's gunny sack in tatters,
as befits a tired man on a journey
he walks through the desert of a dream.
I rock myself a couple of times in the rocking chair.
I sneak a look out the window through the slats of the blinds.
Still on the top of the mailbox,
like a still-standing red symbol of Communism,
a flag is stuck out obstinately.
His letter hasn't arrived yet.
In a space between two in the afternoon,
yet, after adding that rather hopeful adverb,
I return to the rocking chair.
In a round sphere, I roll up my body smaller and smaller.
Like in Mother's womb,
I am practicing going back to that day unimpaired.
I shall be reborn. All the ties I have
registered up to this point will be torn apart and I shall recreate it,
choosing only the what its who call often and write often.
From the torn register,
they are all cackling loudly and you
are also in among them as well.

TRANSLATED BY EUNHWA CHOE

Hye Young Hahn is a winner of the New Writer Award from the *Joong-Ang Daily* and the Youth Novel category Award from Kye-Mong publishers. Hahn has authored a novel, *Soy Bean Paste Cooking Woman*, two children's books: *Sweet William* and *Train to New York*, and a volume of poetry, *A Dry Cleaner Ironing the Pacific Ocean*.

Soon Tae Song

Transfer

When attempting to extract long-rooted feet
Bit by bit, some entangled ties are broken
It even revealed pale grief of deep severances.
Quietly shook off the dirt, in order to walk
Past needed to be shaken off and the land would be forgotten for
    a while.

Without loneliness, how can I trod the new land
The ones refusing to fall by the wind, shrunk themselves
And over every hill, we persevered by whistling and crying
The broken twigs burned themselves
The burned twigs falling and even though its heat became ashes
    in grief,
With the ashes applied to the wound, the roots walked on.

In the beginning, everyone doubted the crossing of the ocean.
We are becoming forest again in the vast land.
Re-rooting the feet was another kind of pain, but,
The countless fine root hair took hold of the dry land in a firm
    grip like native soil.
When embraced in warmth even sand became fertile land.

Ah! Now we are well-united transferred forest.
In here all young trees are not afraid to walk
Everyone found its own place
And is becoming another dense forest.

Winter Star

On winter nights
People don't look up to the stars

In the evening when the world is enveloped by cold
People who lie
Under a low roof, in low temperatures
Cannot look at the stars

When even the hearts have turned into winter
The ones who turnover heartlessly
Cannot cope with the starlight

In order to be able to look up to the star
Either one has to know how to be lonely as the stars
Or remain constant like the stars
Or like the stars shine even in the darkness

As stars are not afraid of cold
One cannot be afraid to
Stand by oneself in the cold winter nights
Under the bare sky
Withstand the cold with the bare body
And be able to talk with the stars

On a cold winter night
To those who look up to the sky
The winter star
It shines
Higher and brighter

Dust

I have
always disregarded you, your lightness,
like what most people think I, too,
thought very light of you.
If I whew and blow away, or
With one wipe of a rag, your existence is eliminated,
I believed cleanliness would be maintained.
But one day
On the dry flowers, between the slats of the mini-blinds,
After seeing you persevere through endless battles of dusting,
I realized that the world is not flat plane
for maintaining cleanness.
But there are corners and shadowed areas and unseen places,
Every time I wipe you away you,
Have casually ridiculed me from the unseen spots.
And I know you have lived with me, from where my hand cannot reach
Before your existence, which can be neglected.
The world is not a place where someone is better than another.
Even in the stars of the universe,
Where you exist in layers of layers and have kept the ancient time
And have existed even before me.
I, myself, am inevitably a particle of this universe, the same
existence as you, Persevering fragilely and I accepted
the reality of it. Ultimately,
your lightness, as the result of weighty death,
and as the certain start of the forever, is recognized.
When it is realized that my existence's irreverence, transience, and limitedness,
Denying your existence is impossible.
In all the gaps in my life, I had to allow your cohabitation,
Before my short life disintegrates,
And become lighter than you.

Television

I know you very well
Your life spent crying and laughing on a bright stage
I know that's all acting
When the camera closes up on your tear-streaming face
I smile while pondering the heart of the expression
On the pupils of your smiling eyes
Seeing the mechanism's careless spotlight, I cluck my tongue
It is certain that you could guess how I know you very well
Therefore you practice in sweat and try to transform but
Since you don't know anything about me you are always apprehensive
The exposed ones are always afraid of the hidden ones
You anxiously act and act
You already know the emptiness of the popularity
If a small flaw of acting is exposed
Your stage can disappear from the screen
Forever not put on the air
Therefore I once thought I could be your ruler
In my innocent days
But I couldn't make you disappear
Rather I am called out every evening
I have to see you act
If I don't I am afraid I will be shunned from this idiot world
Only just recently have I realized that I am
an unpaid extra audience
It is going in a certain
Wrong direction.

Photograph

A friend who died years ago
Is chuckling on the surface of a phosphorescent paper.
While grabbing the shoulders of the very alive me,
He is conspiring double suicide.
As if life were also casting its layer off, within an album,
It is collected as markings of one era.
Is the evaporated time the truth or fabrication.
Why has the time left forever's shard
Awkwardly on the surface of a mere layer of paper.
How life carved in suffering became fermented.
Rather than in reality, the friend smiles only in the splendor of death.
Upon seeing me,
Who can't seem to cope with the unbreakable embrace of the shoulders,
He once again chuckles with a face now much younger than mine.
Even though no sound can be heard,
Bottom of my heart shakes.
The impertinent one. Even if pressed with a finger
The laugh doesn't smear off and doesn't seem like it will stop.
Have I died or has he died
It's hard to distinguish.

TRANSLATED BY EUNHWA CHOE

Soon Tae Song, a member of the Korean Chapter of the International P.E.N. Club, has published two volumes of poetry: *Quivering Forest* and *To the Nameless Names*.

Mee Soon Bae

Canvas

Every night I face you
To beseech you
The purpose of
This crippling agony.

No condensation of dawn
Or luster of moon can
Cure me

Only if I can heave
The hem of
Life's tribulation at you.

With a daring attempt
I extract the essence of
Red, yellow, blue
Relying on unbound
Imagination for
Composition

I unleash myself
Aspiring to gain another self

With tinge of pleasure
I watch myself struggling in
A two-dimensional world.

POETRY

Eulogy to Women
—Woman to Woman

His rib
Made you stronger
Than he
Who is erected from clay

Surpassing maturity be 2-3 years
Enduring longer by 7-8 years
Of him who is erected from clay

Balmy as eiderdown
Profound yet transparent

Your mind is clearer than a jellyfish
Yet impenetrable as a solid diamond
No needle dares to prick you.

Excavating for life
Proclaiming one world after another.
Exchanging love
For pain
A gemstone
How precious is your
Brilliance.

TRANSLATED BY HA YOUNG SHIN

Mee Soon Bae, an editorial writer for the *Korea Daily* in Chicago and director of the Korea Central Culture Center, has published two poetry books: *We Are Flying Away* and *Grass Seeds and Pebbles*.

Yong Chin Chong

Holding up High
the Torch of Korea's Spirit
—Dedicated to the 100 years of Korean immigration

When the fatherland
went through the thorny road,
you too chose the
rough way of a pioneer.

102 grandfathers,
with the nation's spite in their hearts,
cast anchors
in the Hawaiian sugar cane fields
on January 13, 1903.

And you were rooting
at the new continent of America,
shedding the immigrant's grief,
agony and tears.

"I have engraved
deep, deep in my mind
the independence of Korea,
eating
or sleeping
till I die,"
like the bible of a nation,
the pioneer of our nation.

Being pricked and bled,
you picked the oranges
and sweated in the sugar cane field
with those rough hands;

and those funds
you donated for the independence.
At last, we have regained
the independence of the fatherland.

You are
the soul of the nation
the power of the nation
and the root of the nation.

Today,
the day marking 100 years of immigration,
we give you
that joy,
impression,
and glory,
so you deserve to be highlighted.

We all are the gleaming descendents of
Kyung-Chon-Ae-Inn (meaning "respecting God and loving people")
and Hong-Ik-Inn-Gahn (meaning "of broad benefit to the people.")

We, dedicating your intention,
will widen the land of faith,
wisdom and economy
and strengthen
our nation's power
in this wide and young continent.

Now, we'll reunite
our divided fatherland
as one nation,
and we dedicate
a drink in celebration

to you.

We all are
the soul of Korea,
the dream of Korea,
the consanguinity of Korea,
so we'll sing loudly
the song of victory.

TRANSLATED BY SUNG Y. YI

Yong Chin Chong is president and director of the Korean Literary Society of America, an advisor to the Orange Writers Group, and a member of the poet group, The Chipyongson. Chong's poetry books are *River Village*, *At the Rose Field*, and *Filling the Empty Heart with Peace*. His essay books are *Planting the Meaning of Life* and *A Poet and a Farmer*.

Moon Hee Kim

Magnolia

Even if it is bloomed
It is not fully opened.

Even a flower petal
does not carelessly move.

Supported by heavy flower petals
the fragrance spread out
while not fully opened.

At the end of lonely branch,
cliff reaching the sky,
our love has been hidden
oh, it is the grace.

The flowers teach us:
joy should not be light
and
sorrow should be aesthetic.

The flowers open and close
without any word.

TRANSLATED BY YEARN HONG CHOI

Grafting

although a young branch is cut
and inserted into another stem
curiously,
it bears much better fruit
in spite of the cruel cut.

for an immigrant who left
the beloved place, time
and life,

who knows
a keen immigrant's life would also bear
much better fruit
at the end of a branch
that loses its voice
longing for the root?

TRANSLATED BY PAUL LEE

May's Sunlight

May is good
enough with sunlight,

Spring landscape in our hometown
is miraged in milk-lit sunlight.
I miss so many friends
in May.

Despair in the winter
changes into a hope
in May's sunlight

Everything in this foreign place
becomes neat and cozy
to foreigners.

Sunlight in May
makes the forget-me-not bloom
like teething,
like bodyache.

TRANSLATED BY YEARN HONG CHOI

Moon Hee Kim, a former president of the Korean-American Christian Literature Association and the Korean Poets Association of America, has published four poetry books: *Leaves of Grass, Awakening, Autumn River, Morning Grass*, and *Deepening Spirit*. Kim is also a Montessori school principal and a talk-show host on Radio Korea in Los Angeles, where she discusses literary affairs.

William D. Chun

An Alien's Elegance I

I sit on the street and appreciate life;
I become similar to a bull's smile.

You come together from the ends of the earth;
You are Jamaicans or West Indians;
You are Spanish, Italians, or Mexicans;
You are Chinese and Japanese of the Oriental blood relatives;
I am a Korean.

The streets of New York are the demonstration places of all
    human races,
Become rains and drops on the painful loss of the homeland.
I am a poor stranger
whose pupils look toward life
Read life as turning pages
God, please,
Bless me.

An Alien's Elegance II

On the street I smile idiotically on races
Who pass by me brushing collars.

Here is Harlem of Black Power
It made New York, the first city of the world
Called the horrible maternity ward.

To these who are now relieved
Their Uncle Tom's Negro Spirituals and
Harlem's execrations appealing as crying
and then smile mildly:

God, Please
Give the power to live.
Give the power to live.

However, Homeland Is in Spring Yet
—A Diary of YN

The road under the below-zero,
Where the warm stream of breath of the sun
Could not shield my soul.

At the approach of a subway
Where I was pushed by crowds and come here,
Where does the pain of the home-lost man
Who looks at the bright sky
And resembles the behavior of a deaf remains

However, Homeland is in spring yet.

Afternoon that slept on the back of a dog.
Gets deeper in red,
Romantic gives warm hand
Over nature,
Where does the safety of a home-lost man
Who chews fretfulness
Gets a rest?

However, Homeland is in spring yet.

At 5 p.m.
The ennui of everyday life that has passed one process
Buries a heavy body that is rolled by a foreign language,
With maggoli of the homeland bar where I drink occasionally,
I ruminate that there is hometown, and homeland
Even to me with a smile of an ox.

And I drink to life of one day that gets mixed up with
Cruelty, agony, and self-torture.
I drink myself into a state that is denser than blood.

However, Homeland is in spring yet.

TRANSLATED BY JIN KOK KIM

William D. Chun, president of the International P.E.N. Korea Center/USA Division, debuted in *Sim Sang* magazine and authored *The Breath of an Island*.

Sunghee Cho

Long Weekend

All empty
No waving wind, no swaying shadow
All images stopped there like an old picture
Who came and took so many people?
The empty plaza is clear and quiet like a prism

The souls are buried in our stories, and where are the bare bodies, hanging like the frogs
in a specimen room? The fragrant wild roses, hanging upside down like a cross, must
have become white straws. Who came and ate all sweet and sappy, wild-rose stems, and
took away my girl, leaving an empty forest? The plum-colored sunset hangs on the forest
and makes me fall asleep in strange edge between this and that life.

On the last day, when the solitude comes after you and me, the love I wore will slide
down like a cast-off skin and add one small dot on the traces of the sand, the wind, and
the stars.

Empty city, empty hours of long weekend
Is as faint as my dusky hometown beach of seabirds' eggs and their rolling footprints.

POETRY

Shadow Reading

A space too loose to call a body
Yet too desolate to call a space
On those wings I push away and keep
Being and not being
I fell asleep along with all the swaying things
Gently

TRANSLATED BY ELSIE HYERYUNG KIM

Sunghee Cho, former president of the Korean Poets' Association of America, has published poetry collections, including *Extracting a Tooth* and *One Small Dot Shattering into Bits and Bits*.

Chungmi Kim

Brother

I

Brother
you left your Ma
your children
your woman
back in Korea.

America is no paradise
you've found out.

You are silent
with no rolling tongue.
You are crippled
with no four-wheeled legs.
And
you poison
yourself
with regrets.

Cry aloud if you can.
I know you won't.
Instead
you hide and
drown in cigarette smoke.

Sorry
you spilled the ash
by my door yesterday.
Otherwise
I would not have cried

for you.

II

My Brother
slouching your body
lean and weary
you do not jump or sing
like you used to.

I took you out
to my apple tree
last Sunday afternoon.

The sun was high
hidden
behind the cloud screen.

Clinging
to a willowy branch
you chopped and sawed the branches
reaching high to the sky.

Quivering
like a bow against an arrow
you were a leopard
I imagined.

Pour out the stifled breath
of your old memories.
Let it drift away
to be the rainfall
in the far away forest.

Mutilated

SURFACING SADNESS

the apple tree we meant to shape
stood
dumb and crippled.

You said you were sorry
the tree might die.
I said gladly
the tree will survive.

Returning

Thoughts are nurtured
by the touch of my soul.

Born out of thoughts
words are made to be beads.

I string them to capture
the memories of time spent
in this life

returning

somewhere in the universe
to be imprinted in the void
like stars.

Off to the Grammys

The day at last came
to go
to the Grammys.

With a borrowed mink coat
and a yellow flower
pinned
on my black silk dress
I walked
like a star
escorted by my man.

Glittering lights
blinding my eyes
I heard the crowd
shouting
as a limousine pulled in.
A Star.
A woman in a slinky outfit
slid
like a rattle snake
a smile
pasted like a toothpaste
commercial.

The auditorium was full
with diamonds and silks
tuxedoes and bare shoulders.
Amongst the shouts and whispers
I sat invisible
sunk
in my own fantasy.

Show biz.

Thousands of dreamers gathered
together in a feast
no one saying hello
perfect strangers exchanging
nothing but prepared smiles.

Glossy painted-faces floated
the music was rocking
the crowd was stomping
crushing
stepping on the flowers.

Spotlights rampant
food plenty
it was the night to go mad.

Ah, why did I ever dream of
stardom?

A pale moon I was
quietly
content to stay
behind.

I am

A container
I am
empty
for seasons of many
longing souls.
A dreamer
I am
aloof
floating
timelessly.

Question me
no more
where I come
from
where I must
go
between
East and West.

Vapor
I am
no one can
catch
the presence
in a grasp.

Homeless
I am
rootless

I am
free
as the summer
clouds

carrying home
wherever
I
go.

Chungmi Kim, a poet and playwright, is the author of *Chungmi-Selected Poems*. *Hanako*, her full-length play about Korean comfort women, premiered at East-West Players in Los Angeles in 1999. The *Los Angeles Times* selected Kim as one of the "Faces to Watch in 1999."

Chang Yun Lee

Daily Bread

Finally in my late years
I learn to bow before the breakfast table.

In a dusty, wild plain, the Son of Man is walking
In his footsteps, there follow twelve stalwart men
It is a Sabbath, how hungry they must be
Look at the hand that crumbles a wheat spike into his mouth
How big it is! The two guilty hands
Hiding under the outer coat can be seen.

Give us this day our daily bread
—Give us, the whisper of the prayer by the Son of Man can be heard
He would know
Two thousand years later a hotel would be built on that road
On a plastic card there will not be JESUS CHRIST
But even if a humble name like mine is engraved
A miracle so unlike a miracle occurs.

Bowing my head before the breakfast table
I close my eyes for a moment
In the dusty road, the Son of Man is walking
In the hunger lingering Middle Eastern sky
An egg yolk like sun floats
His sandals are like two pieces of toast
Worn thin.

Sky Above the Orchard

After planting three apple trees
In the back yard
I look up at the sky above the orchard.

Above your orchard still hangs
My autumn sky
Listening to your younger voice calling me
Answering in my young voice
While the summer passes
Like the crabapples burning black
Into that sky
Endlessly going far away.

Even at the age past sixty
The things I yearn for still remain
That sky's rim is
Suddenly fading away.

TRANSLATED BY EUNHWA CHOE

Chang Yun Lee, a medical doctor and professor of medicine in Detroit, has published two volumes of poetry, *Leaves' Coast* and *Even Though the River Flows from Afar*.

Samuel Changhyun Yim

Father and Seal

Everyone lives with a seal carved in wood, stone, or horn,
Flesh is chiseled. Bones are engraved in this world.
Since people do not trust each other,
I spent some 20 years stamping the seal on my behalf.
When I stamped the seal, the seal stamped me.
I have nowhere to use this seal any longer.
Time and again I stamped it,
But all it stamped is yesterday, the memories at best.
I no longer have any piece of land to sell or buy,
Nor any deal to be confirmed with this seal.
Sometimes I stamp the book of my poems
With an ivory seal worn out where the fingers touch,
Without much thought out of my old habit.
I remember my father's seal.
It fascinated me so much
That I stamped on paper stealthily.
Today I became a father, but...
My son does not get fascinated by my seal.
Probably because he is living in a world
Where the seal is no longer in use.
However hard you stamp it,
Its marks do not confirm our belief nor the right of possession.
Now I impress my seal and my father's old crystal seal alternately,
On a piece of white paper, and find that
My father's seal seems much more powerful than mine.
But he is at last deeply in sleep now,
After he sealed the land with his own body.
And I find myself stamping my memory
In an empty sky that does not hold my yearning.

And the Day After

On September 11, 2001
I was walking under the trees in Yosemite,
When I heard the terrifying story from my children
That a seven-year-old cucumber
Flew over to America.
Four million tons of 220 stories,
The trunk of New York City
Tumbled down like a waterfall.
A Niagara Falls, with American blood
Falling down instead of water.
It was indeed the Armageddon of the 21st century.
Can the tons of tears emptying out of 200 million souls
Save a single life?

So much lost, so many tears.

And then afterward the airports were closed.
I drove along the San Francisco bay,
Then walked down the beautiful Pebble Beach
Stretching out over some 17 miles.
Lonely, I felt like a pine tree
Standing on the steep cliff there.
Oh, the sense of emptiness in the heart,
When I realized that God was not there.
I saw a boy and an old man standing,
Waving the Stars and Stripes on the hill
Caressed by the waves crashed from the sea.
I could not help it, and tears ran
Down the cheeks like waves.

Justina's voice from the recorded tape hit my eardrum.
She is a Korean girl, an attorney of
Only twenty-eight years young, who said:
"Mom, I saw an airplane fly toward me and crash."

SURFACING SADNESS

Oh, what a final confirmation
Between mother and daughter.

Beautiful is the human being, the fact that
One is alive.
So was the exchange of words:
"I love you, Mom."
"I love you, Honey."

TRANSLATED BY SUN MYUNG LEE

Samuel Changhyun Yim, a former president and an organizing member of the Korean Poets and Writers Association, published *Again and Again* (1997), *My Memories Are Not for Sale* (2000), and *The Washington Pensees* (2001). His essay collection includes *Agonies of Life* (1988) and *Practice Parting* (1993).

Hye Shin Lim

Cold Medicine

Baby, don't cry, you don't have to suffer through cold any more
Let's drink up a spoonful of grape-hued medicine

Then mommy doesn't have to be envious again
Love in the love's chest
Sorrow in the sorrow's chest shut
You and I shall live in the clear and sturdy marble on the top of the chest

Baby, don't cry, let us go over the mountain
Where even without desire lovers are strong
Where even without sunlight lawn is green
Remove the bed, remove the sofa, remove the computer
In a large, very large house with only a new specie of dog
That would lick the back of your hand, let us go there

Baby, don't cough, where with one medicine a thousand illnesses could be cured
Where time expands and shrinks like rubber
We are almost there

Once there, we could take a walk in a few hundred years in the darkness
And splash around in the starlight for a thousand years and wonder what pain is
What is dream? What is mommy?
And after looking down on the dark planets in thought

SURFACING SADNESS

When bells tinkle from somewhere
Where one could sleep as in love and feather, let us go to that new land

Yes, you are very patient. My pretty baby
But what shall we call the exciting land?
Padipa, Palace of Disappeared Pain?
Hedipa, Heaven of Disappeared Sorrow?
If not, just have a series
And call it, This Life 1, This Life 2, or This Life 3?

TRANSLATED BY EUNHWA CHOE

Worn Wooden Pier

On the days when I yearn for you
even on the days I don't yearn for you
I still go out to the sea.
The scattering wind by the sunlight's clear tune.
Starting small like a hand wave of Hi!
and growing big as a sailboat,
the sea, which at once breaks down like a mountain,
enables me to discard you.

The yearning disappears into light waves.
The wandering desire crumbles into brilliance like sand.

Under the sun that throws its body like a harpoon,
the fact that the love should be hot and
the fact that the life should be beautiful are being forgotten.

On bare feet and with bare hands,
when I step on your blue cloth,
the deep sea's ribs would open.
"Hope, memory, freedom, pain..." words like these
"Spoon, pot, steel chain, hoe..." words like these
full within me undulates and I
become your interior.

Therefore, that dangerous and smooth,
between you and I,
only the worn wooden pathway
remains and flows.

TRANSLATED BY EUNHWA CHOE

A Woman Worker Eating a Mango

When she looks up,
it is only the sky
burning on the hot terrain.
In her blue gown,
she walks to hidden shade,
opens a brown bag, then
there is a mango bouncing out
like a wildflower just blooming.

A short freedom,
a hovering wind among butterflies
disappears into a sip of juice.

"Life can be sweet
once in a while,"
as their conversations flow
up the reddish stairs and
pass through grass fields
and to the melting horizon.

The pouring tiredness
in the afternoon slips away
with such a brief
kiss in the shadow of
a juicy bite of mango.

TRANSLATED BY HYE SHIN LIM

Hye Shin Lim is a winner of the New Poet's and Writer's Award from the Washington Korean Poets and Writers Association, and the Annual Poetry Award from the *Los Angeles Korea Times*. Lim published her first book of poems, *Forest of Illusions*, in 2001.

Kwi Soon Kwon

Apricot Blossom

No one is hurrying.
The winter wood has not spoken a word.
The southern winds have not told us,
Winter is not over.
But the apricot is blossoming
At the bottom of the mountain.
Buds are tense
Just like the bullets
Before firing.
The apricot blossoms after breeze.
Apricot blossom, apricot blossom.
The bees sit in the apricot flowers.
Who blames the bees for kissing the blossom
All day long?
Apricot blossom; apricot blossom.

Evening Birds

I don't know
Whether birds know about the sunset.
I don't know
Whether birds know the sorrow
Created by the dusk.
Birds' cry shaking the evening sky,
Darkness creeping the sunset glow,
A flock of birds soaring up the darkened sky.
I don't know
Whether birds can remember
The passage of time
As the sorrow makes humans sing,
Does the sorrow make the birds sing?
The birds return to the woods.
The naked trees in the winter
Cannot hide anyone's sorrow.
The birds' singing or crying
Shakes the empty woods.
It is strange:
Complete darkness suddenly silences the birds.
I cannot see a single bird
Nor can I hear any chirp.
I don't know
Whether my life is a kind of sorrow
Silenced in the darkened woods.

Sleep on the Fallen Leaves

Sleep on the fallen leaves!

Under an oak tree,
Lay down your body
On the leaves, and
Blanket your soul
With fallen leaves.

Forget the world, time, neighbors,
And money.
You will realize that
Your body is light like feather,
Soon will return to the earth
As the leaves return to the root.

You will count the stars
In the sky,
And you will see new stars, stars
You have never seen before.

The most beautiful dream will come
Into sleep.

TRANSLATED BY YEARN HONG CHOI

Kwi Soon Kwon, a member of the Fragrance of Poetry, is a winner of the *Korean P.E.N. Magazine*, and a winner of the Washington Poets and Writers' Award.

Soon Paik

Spring Rain

In the middle of the night
Spring rain knocks against glass ceiling.

Sprouting up shoots
Out of the bark of the winter tree and
Bringing up pains from
Across the ocean.

Green sprout spread
In the field toward the Blue Ridge Mountains,
Yet winter winds of sorrow's lingering cold
With a longing toward home country.

Land divided,
Living deteriorated and
Love lost.

In the backyard and
the streets of the town
Spring has come with the opening of flower bud,

Yet spring is afar in my soul.
The spring rain taps on the window of my heart
long waiting
For the delayed spring.

Rain Drops

Embracing wife, moaning with high fever
On the way to the emergency room
As if pounding a sorrowful heart
The raindrops tap the windshield

Light lucid by the raindrops
Reflects early days in West Virginia.

The sound of rain knocking on the window
Is melodious in tune
to a voice of heaven.

Leaving wife, sleeping well in the hospital
On the way home
the raindrops still tap the windshield

Pounding strongly the window of my heart
Awakening a depressed spirit
Making a chorus of thanksgiving.

Raindrops are love
and the source of life.

Sound of Autumn

Is it the sound of wind
Blowing away fallen leaves
Containing spring's hopes and dreams
On the yellowing grass lawn?

Is it the sound of breath of nature
Converting the summer's prosperous forest
Along the Potomac River?

Yes, it is the cry of a cricket in the backyard
Resembling mother's friendly call
From the kitchen
"Dinner is ready."

It is the chatter of silence
Travelling across the Pacific Ocean
Originated from father's tomb in North Korea
"I want to go home."

It is a whisper of heart
Echoing along Appalachian Mountain Track
"I am a love."

Resurrection

From between the tree branch in the backyard
with the sound of the birds
Comes the morning of the resurrection.

Azalea budding along the Potomac River
heralds the Spring's coming maturity
discreetly and elegantly.

The Christian chorus before the Jefferson Memorial
is spreading the grace of the Lord to the world.
The morning of the resurrection is coming.

Across the ocean
on the divided peninsula
The resurrecting morning
that will calm the half century
of separated families' grief.

TRANSLATED BY YEARN HONG CHOI

Annapolis

On a pier in Annapolis
standing alone
enjoying the wind from the sea.

A wind carrying a smell of Western civilization
Across the Atlantic Ocean
Blows my brunette, not golden, hair.

With my body, my clothes and my shoes
Full of Western lifestyle
I walk boastfully
On the market place in Annapolis.

Knowing the tide will erase it
I scribe my name in Korean
On the Annapolis beach
and ask to the waves.

How long will my son and his descendents
Keep their names in Korean?

Soon Paik is the author of the poetry anthology *And the Lord's Love Overflows*, has won New Poet Awards from *Korean Expatriate Literature* and *JaYu Literature*, as well as a New Essayist Award in Korean language literature, and has published a collection of religious poems in Korean.

Ryang Suh

Fried Locusts

The heads of the rice were drooping laxly
on the levee of grassy forest in a golden rice paddy.
I used to catch the locusts
leaping like jumpy life.
On occasion I would let go of the autumn
when I get to grab the brownish dirty liquid-like ones,
the so-called "dead-body locusts."

Inside the blue soda bottle
during the starving night,
the locusts would defecate massively.

In the squeaky clean mirror
scrubbed with fragrant soap and water,
I am eating locusts with no dung.
Yummy, crunchy, well soaked in the sesame oil,
the fried locusts give out
savory happiness of the autumn.

The heads of the rice are still swaying
after the locusts leaped flying away.
The silky blue collars of their clothes
tickle the palm of my hand, love dappling
the rainbow-colored antennae of theirs,
slowly, very slowly fading away
like torrid dusk in the autumn.

SURFACING SADNESS

Bear Mountain Sonata

I'd like it to be as it is:
Everything totally the way we are.

The mountaintop that wanes slowly;
the mass of the moon that presses the clouds;
and the sensation of the touch on the supple fog:
All these things totally
as if to be as it is.

The mountain is singing louder and louder.
Our miniscule temperature scatters around
in the wind whirling through the valleys,
as if to be as it is.

You and I, the flow of our consciousness is
a melody of sorrow sung beautifully,
keeping our shoulder blades aflutter
in such a good harmonic progression of the universe
undulating in the fog on the floor of the mountain:
Like the moan of the wind
dying Bear Mountain spews.

I'd really like it to be as it is.

Ryang Suh, a psychiatrist, is a former vice president of the Korean Writers Association of East America and has published his selected poems in *The Theater Troupe of Manhattan*.

Young Kyo Kim

Traffic Lights

Traffic lights are dad's face
Day and night
Watching over me from high above.

The face with green light smiling on me
Is a generous praise
For what I've done right.

Sometimes his face turns hysterical yellow
warning out of worries
Against a possible mishap.

Now away with ever-present
Compliments and concerns
Dad gets angry showing red on his face.
Then realizing for sure I am against his will
I come to a complete stop right away
And examine myself for the safety.

Nights fall on the middle of an intersection
Yet, I find myself smoothly moving
As the lights command, (for I can read Dad's face)

Now, on the crossroads in my life
I find no lights of fear
Because Dad's love is the signal
Through the green path of life
To move on straight forward
In the right direction of the traffic flows.

Music

When I'm with you
A muddy stream turns to crystal water
And merging into a river,
then flows deep within me.

When I'm with you
A rock-hard heart becomes
A bird, feather-light and
flying high in the wind
above the boundless sky.

When I'm with you
A frozen winter bulb turns
Into a flower in full blossom
Smiling in the caress of spring air.

Many times, I yearn
To be a fish swimming free in the ocean,
To be the pupils of a bird's-eye view, and
To be the sweet aroma of spring flowers which travels afar.

Upon embracing the sky with stars shining smile,
Being captured with the joy indulgence
The eyes settle down in the nest of your bosom,
Giving birth to a heavenly universe
With the wings wide open,
And now promise spectacular flights of tomorrow.

Young Kyo Kim, executive director of both the Korean-American Poets Association and the Korean-American Literary Association, is the recipient of the Eighth Andes Literary Award. Her publications include *Quartet of Afternoon, Vols. 1 and 2*, *Songs of Hyssop*, *Traffic Lights,* and *Crying Stone*.

Duk Jae Shin

You, Go to Alaska to Get Aurora Down in Your Palm

I
You go to Alaska to get Aurora down
In your palm

The arctic land, Alaska:
The barren horizon there stretches

Its icy serrate winds over frozen land.
The snow avalanches for it rumble down
Rushing in frozen seas all the year round,
As if an eternal tragedy of clashes
Of an iced land echoed through the vast
Solitariness in white winter's soul
Forever to cry.

And you go to Alaska to get
Aurora down in your palm.

The sharpened screeching sounds
Of winds all night through, battering:
It may threaten you to be frozen off
In the forty miles up north of Eskimo's
Silence of an iced home of igloo,
Through serrate winds, you will remember
You still keep awakened consciously
Over the white night, for your regaining
Spirit for life, the life you do not wish
To lose in the arctic extremes

II

But icy, bladed chills piercing you by,
Shivered, gaining fiercer, through sweeping
Arctic howls, you may strongly feel that,
If lived, you would bear out your dream
Of growing green Alaskan willow in you
And in your aching heart to resist
The freezing colds of the Arctic land.

You, now open your heart widely
And you discard your disputable
Idealism away in Alaska
And then, let your overwhelmed
Yearning for the primitive Alaska
Wander in your soul to search
For the last one of survival.

You, let you go to Alaska
the Arctic primitive land
You, let you go to Alaska
The Arctic untrodden land

III

You, go to Alaska to get Aurora down
In your palm, and to see Aurora flower
Far off horizon; calling you
From where you stand, and calling you
From where a herd of winter bull moose
Gather together to become your friends
And where a gasping breath of death

In the fiery January becomes your last
Friend to be intimate.

And there, you can hear the reverberating
Breaks for iced depth of frozen rivers
Echoing in your soul over the dead land.

You, my friend, go to Alaska to get
Aurora down in your palm,
And hear the passion of freezing winds
There, the Alaskan cries, chilling
Its horizon far off,
And you, to eternal awake.

Duk Jae Shin, a recipient of the New Poet Award from *Echo* magazine and a resident of Garland, Texas, is a member of the Korean-American Literary Society.

ESSAYS

Dae Wook Chang

At a Grocery Store

COMPARED TO TODAY'S grocery store, the size of the grocery store was smaller then, and usually had a small office near the counter. Depending on the store, it provided some banking services to the customers. I don't think they do this any more, but back then, the store would also cash small personal checks from a window of the office.

One day, the cashed money was no less than a twenty-dollar bill. Holding on to the "big bill," I went over to the cashier's line, where my wife was waiting in the line. I handed her the twenty-dollar bill and waited for the grocery bags to be filled.

That was when a gentleman tapped my shoulder and motioned to follow him. He pulled my hand and asked how I could hand over a large bill like that to my wife, as if it were the most unbelievably strange thing. I had no idea what the deal was until he asked how I could do that when twenty dollars was a large sum of money. "It's alright if it's meant to educate your wife," he said.

I, in turn, was flabbergasted by his use of the word "educate." The one who lectured about money was my wife, not I. It didn't happen just yesterday or today, but all our lives. I was not certain, but I believed the gentleman was of Jewish descent.

This happened again at the same store. It was a day in a spring, when I went over to the aforementioned window to cash a small check from the state-tax refund. I was going to shop for groceries with that money. I submitted the check from the state treasury, and asked whether it could be cashed even though it wasn't a personal check. But the woman in the window neither acknowledged me, nor listened to what I was saying. Instead, she just kept on tapping the bulletin board next to the window. It probably meant that the board had the explanation.

However, I already knew that information. Since I didn't quite understand, I asked her again. The response from her was the same except the tapping became stronger. It meant "you still don't know."

"Listen! I am a customer too. How can you treat me like this when we are all same customers."

I wanted to complain this way, but I figured a white person wouldn't behave in this manner so I refrained myself. In any event, my broken English came out rather smoothly and in the meantime there was a change in her. "No! It's not the money. The problem is the way of your talking!" she said. The customers behind me were standing with a look of "none of my business." Perhaps that was the reason she left the store soon after. A while after the incident, I ran across her at another store where she worked as a cashier. She looked elsewhere without lifting her face and in turn, I walked away without acknowledging her.

TRANSLATED BY EUNHWA CHOE

The late **Dae Wook Chang** has published three books: *History of Korean-American Churches in Washington, D.C., Dual Citizenship,* and *With the Wind and the Times.*

Ke Hyang Lee

By the Window

I HAVE LOST all sense of time. On this night—the longest of the year—I find myself standing at my favorite window, which just a few hours ago framed the setting sun. Now, in the pitch dark, I gaze at the woods not far from my apartment building.

Although it is virtually impossible to see anything in this densely thicketed woods, I have a sense of the various activities going on within. I know that birds sleep in their nests; that squirrels, chipmunks, and other small rodents have returned to their various homes; that owls on high perches watch for small creatures bound on their night-life who will become their prey.

The darkness stretches upward from my familiar woods like a black velvet curtain. I know it is not a curtain, for it reaches not only upward but in all directions. An airplane, majestic even at such a distance, flies on its scheduled route, demonstrating to me the ongoing dimensions of the darkness. At yet a greater distance, when clouds do not interpose, one sights the moon and the stars.

Above it all, does some keen eye, some greater mind look back at me through the darkness with inner rapport that reads my troubled thoughts and feels the depth of my joy? I wonder if my life is also as transparent as this window, and if my innermost being can be seen and heard in spite of my seemingly inaudible and unseen lifestyle.

The window has been my best friend for fourteen long years. We've been through everything together, both joy and pain. When I feel discouraged or distressed, when I have something wonderful to share, it has been my habit to stand by the window and talk. The window remains a silent partner, merely listening and sharing my thoughts and feelings. It has proved over and over again to be a faithful and confidential companion with no human malice or betrayal.

I must admit that at times I have been discouraged by the silent response and lack of reaction I receive from the window. My window seems to watch me with compassion and understanding, but being a vain and helpless human, at times I need tangible evidence that it cares for me. I need a strong reminder that I flow with the human current. I need a human touch in order to feel alive and functional. However, I certainly do not feel dead or dysfunctional because I receive no demonstrable evidence of affection from my best friend, my westward window.

At one particular stage of my life, I was keenly aware that I must find some means of supporting myself. Before mingling with the tide of humanity, those who had found their places among the self supporting and those who were still seeking, I spent an amazing amount of time standing at the window, awaiting advice and direction, which I embraced, in spite of its unspoken quality, as if it were handed to me by a great sage. Perhaps my ardor in seeking advice from my window was in exact proportion to the dread I felt as I thought of joining that throng.

After inquiring in every one of the countless nooks and crannies of each street, I was still without employment. It was a humiliating and humbling experience for me, learning the importance of being alive. While I was pushed and pulled by this walking tide of humanity, I bitterly admitted how insignificant and fragile my existence—less than a bubble—as I returned home like a defeated soldier, exhausted physically and mentally from the battle ground. Even before I propped down on the chair, my battered soul sought refuge at the window.

I was received with the usual silence. No word was spoken, yet I was strangely conscious of ever-flowing compassion. With this friend who already knew me inside and out, I had to be honest. I told it of my frustration, disenchantment, and deeply felt sorrow. I wept as I humbly told it all my cares. It embraced me with its warm arms, and I felt much better—as if some weight were lifted from my shoulders.

Now I know and need my westward window more than ever. I know it will always be there for me—all the rainy and sunny days of my life. I have a renewed appreciation for my best friend. I can always return to my solace whenever I am saddened by the hurt inflicted by humanity.

This morning I shall wash my window until it sparkles and then polish it with a silky cloth as if I were handling the most precious treasure under heaven. And perhaps I am. Undoubtedly, to place such meaning upon a simple pane of glass seems ridiculous to some. Why, then, does it mean so much to me?

Because, as it is popular to declaim in certain metaphysical circles, there is an inner child in all of us, a child who is awed by a power that is Father to us all. We feel too microscopically small to kneel, look upon all the vastness of time and space, and empty our souls of all of life's intensities. It is just too overwhelming.

A little child clutches a blanket, a teddy bear, a rag doll. When Mother and Father are not there, this object is a representation of their love. In like manner, each of us needs a symbol through which we are reassured of our Father's love, reminded of His counsel.

My symbol is my window. It brings into my life my beloved woods, the sunlight, the stars, in fact, a cross-section of the universe of which I am a part. These remind me of the Creator of us all. It seems a concrete source of inspiration, which certainly does not come from a pane of glass, any more than such an impersonal object can offer me compassion.

But, like the little child's teddy bear, it is a symbol of some larger, all-encompassing power from which I can accept love, forgiveness, compassion, and wisdom when they come through some simple objects which I have imbued with a special significance, although I know fully well where they really came from. In this way, I can handle the overwhelming awe which shuts me off, overcome by my own insignificance.

On this night, I find myself standing at my favorite window.

SURFACING SADNESS

TRANSLATED BY JIN YOUNG PARK

Ke Hyang Lee, founder of the Korean Writer's Association of America in 1989, has published *The Complete Works of Ke Hyang Lee* in nine volumes.

Wan Soo Byun

The Return of the Prodigal Son

IT'S BEEN EXACTLY twenty years. Coming back home. I have come back to my second home. Walking over the Key Bridge exactly twenty years later. The Potomac River's Key Bridge that connects Washington, D.C. and Arlington, Virginia. I call this place my second home.

If my birthplace of Moon-Kyung in Korea is the place of my life's creation, it suffices to say that District of Columbia and Arlington area is the self-appointed town in the second half of my life. Liking it or not, this is where I began the latter half of my life.

In no time, it's December. At the rush of the year's end, I am standing by the railing of the Key Bridge. At a salt-and-pepper age, as a half-century-spent wayfarer. Should I say, the return of the prodigal son?

The Potomac River is covered in thin ice and the George Washington Memorial Parkway's lingering roadside snow seems chilly. Although the old image of Rosslyn, with its high-rises, cannot be found, on the northern hill, the Georgetown University's steeple still hasn't lost its foreign atmosphere. Ah, underneath it, there's Foxhole Drive. It definitely is it. Suddenly, I could remember the road leading to American University, which I once attended.

The beauty of the scenery during the autumn season when the leaves wrap up the windshield. The pleasure of that time renews as if it were yesterday. The thoughts of the prodigal son, who took advantage of the foreign land's north, south, east, and west, ran unconsciously back twenty years. With the brightening streetlights of the Key Bridge, under the evening haze, the vividly reanimated memories are that of "too flabbergasted to cry or laugh" melancholy, old happenings of the early immigrant years.

SURFACING SADNESS

December 29, 1967. That's the day I arrived in America. In other words, it's my second birth date. Arrived at Dulles Airport through Northwest Airline, thirty-three-year-old bachelor and part-foreign student, six feet tall and 115 pounds. I arrived with 140 dollars in my pocket, protected like the ancestral tablets. The first dwelling was the white-only house, where only whites were supposed to be allowed, in the vicinity. It was a rooming house. The first job was at the China Doll Restaurant in Chinatown. The occupation was waiter. Promoted directly to it without having to be a bus boy. The first day's tip, which was first ever in my life, was a large sum of two quarters.

On that night, in self-made celebration, I spent all that money, and that was the beginning of my riotous, foreign life.

From rooming house to rooming house. From boarding house to an apartment. How many times had I moved from place to place? A janitor to a waiter, a drug store clerk to a hotel houseman. From a Chinese restaurant to an Italian restaurant. At one time, a full-time language instructor to a part-time student. A graveyard shift as a Red Top cabbie. Fired many times and quit many times. It was two years worth of plunging forward on this and dashing in on that.

The most unforgettable tie claiming that period was that of the Key Bridge. During that time, my living revolved around the Key Bridge to the north of the river, Washington, D.C. and to the south of the river, Arlington. Therefore, this bridge was the bridge of survival connecting my dwelling to my occupation. Sometimes I walked up north and sometimes I rode the bus down south. Later, I drove my first love, a Saab, endlessly back and forth. The female spies, who came and went over Im-jin River, couldn't have felt more lonely or weary.

However, it was also a time when compassion existed. It was somewhat romantic as well. With forehead to forehead, I enjoyed eating the Bachelor's recipe, made with canned tuna cooked with green onions and red-pepper flakes or paste, relieving the discomforts of a man away from home. At a poor, foreign student couple's place, feeling at ease, I shared their leftover food and drinks, sprouting friendships which would last more than twenty years. There was also Mrs. Jones, who gave me two used pots and two blankets on the day I first rented an apartment. How can I ever forget the kindness from those blue eyes? If it were the Age of Greed today, it had been the Age of Innocence, twenty years ago.

Lastly, I would like to recollect a piece of old memory. Of course, it has to do with the Key Bridge.

It was December 31, probably in 1968. It was a little after a year after my arrival. It was my second year of immigrant life. I walked over the twilight-drenched Key Bridge. The destination was an Italian restaurant in Georgetown. I was going up north on New Year's eve. It wasn't to meet a young woman. As my calling was as a waiter, I was blessed with a special promotion for the night. On New Year's eve, when I didn't have any place to go, the owner of a restaurant where I used to work gave me an unexpected call for help. I was glad. Shall I call it the salvation of the eve? I was relieved from utter solitude.

The work was over around 11:30 p.m. that night. Since I had collected not a shabby amount of tip, on my way back, I was on a pilgrimage to the bars of the Georgetown. I must have followed the M Street, which leads to the Key Bridge, and stopped by every bar, Martini on the Rocks. One moderated drink per place. However, by the time I reached the Key Bridge, I was probably well drunk by the unbearable homesickness and the strong liquor. I was going down south all alone. "Hwang-sun yet-tuh-ae..." My favorite automatically came out in tune. "...wol-sak-mahn...oh pity, what am I looking for wandering in this endless American land..." It must have been around this time that a car gave a sudden brake. With young folks shouting joy, Auld Lang Syne poured forth. The car was a small convertible.

In December's piercing north wind, it was a convertible car. They were packed like bean sprouts. But what was happening? The next moment, I was on that bean-sprout container. It must be true that I was on someone's knees, no, a foreign woman's knees, but I can't remember what sort of English conversation I had before climbing into that car. And already I was vacantly standing in front of my rooming house and they, as if in a chorus, let out "Happy New Year!" and disappeared into the darkness. I can still clearly hear that sound, that "Happy New Year!"

How could I ever forget what had happened that night! What was more refine and elegant than that? None would exist even in remote antiquity. They say three tops for the New Year's day. On the top of the riverbank, on the top of a bridge, and the voluminous top of the knees, to Auld Lang Syne!

TRANSLATED BY EUNHWA CHOE

Wan Soo Byun, publisher of *Four Seas* quarterly, wrote two monthly columns, "West and East" and "East, West, South, North" in the *Literature Abroad Journal* (*Ool-Lim*) and *Korean-American Life Magazine.*

Jay Sang Rhee

Father and Son

THE FIRST THING I ever wrote about was my father. When it was printed in my middle-school magazine, my mother read it a few times and looked at me proudly. But now, nothing concrete in terms of emotion about my father comes to me. The word "father" is only an abstract noun that feels like the wind at the top of a tree in the sun. Yet, I could not shake the vague and deep longing in my heart.

I lost my father during the Korean War. I was seven by Korean reckoning when I lost him to the North. I have never seen him since, nor was I able to verify whether he was still alive or not. My memory of him barely continues, like an old film. When my mother was pregnant with me, her first one, my father was drafted into the Japanese Army as a student-soldier. He returned home on a boat from China in the year Korea regained its independence, having escaped to Manchuria as a resistance fighter. The four years I spent with him since then were all the time I ever had with him.

Father was a college professor and he always read books in his study. The atmosphere of his study remains in my memory as peaceful as the way he put me down on the green grass. He would turn to look at me from the book that he was reading and open the second-story window. Leaning out, he would pick some chestnuts and give them to me. Once, when I was playing on the steps of our university faculty housing, one of my father's students handed me a gift package. That evening I was severely scolded by my father for having received it. Remembrances of my father are only pieces that do not fit properly.

During our life as refugees, sitting in a rented room was as comfortable as being in a study, as long as we had scrounged up some apple crates and filled them with books. Then I would remember the old days and my father.

When we were about to leave for the United States, I went to visit his hometown. I got a faded photo of him with his Imperial University mortarboard on, which I brought with me and hung in my little study in this foreign land. It had been taken of my father when he was about the same age as our oldest son, though he still looks like an elder to me.

Father was dragged away by people with red armbands. Still, our family was treated as one from which a member had gone north voluntarily. Mother tried to protect us with all her might in place of Father, but I could not free myself from the stigma. Just as soon as demonstrators began to encounter the police, my friends would push me to the rear, concerned about my safety. The Korean Central Intelligence Agency called me in to ask about my personal life in a dignified enough manner, but I was often depressed in my youth owing to the anxiety that I was being watched.

In those days, my father was said to have a position as head librarian at some university in North Korea. I used to tame my anger and frustration by showing the resentment I had against my father to my lonely mother. How sad my mother must have been! I was really an immature son. When I graduated from college, I was assigned as an officer in ROTC. My family then escaped from the anxiety occasioned by our long oppression as relatives of a defector in the North. But my mother clung to her worry that it might mean that my father had died.

But this fear returned again after I got out of the military, and had gotten a job, gotten married, and had a child. One day, when I returned home from work, my whole family was deep in worry. An officer of the local police had come and apparently taken the name, in Chinese character and without missing a stroke, of our child who was barely a year old. My wife was terrified. The fact that our family, which had been suffering from being separated for all this time, had been under their watchful eye, made me shudder. It was at this moment that I decided to emigrate to the United States, even though it meant leaving the job I loved.

Some time ago, some U.C.-Berkeley students hosted a unification conference between North and South Koreas at which representatives from both Koreas participated. The conference site happened to be the community center just across from my store. But I didn't attend it, because they seemed to me to be empty talkers of unification who could not even let me know whether my father was living or not. Furthermore, I did not like my being a spectator in the unification discussion when in fact I was a victim of the division.

Three years ago, I filed an application with the Separated Families Services in Canada, but I have not heard from them yet. Some people have gone to North Korea and successfully met their brothers who had volunteered for the North Korean military, but I am frustrated that I cannot even find out whether my father is alive or not.

While I dearly miss my own father, I have also become a father to my two sons. They say that you can only give as much love as you have received. I had to dig deep into my psyche for the love I had received in my four years with my father. I was unsure of my own fatherhood, and I felt as anxious about it as I do about my old age.

We emigrated to the U.S. when our first child was four years old. One day, when I was returning home, I saw a circle of children standing on the lawn in front of our apartment building. In the middle was a child whom the other American children were pushing and hitting. I ran over and found that the child was my son of short stature. He wasn't just taking it. He stood his ground before his more forceful opponents. When I saw that my son was not crying, I regretted having immigrated to the U.S., for the first time.

But my son began to immerse himself in America when he began attending school. He was deeply interested in the African-American hero, Malcolm X, and read his books and enjoyed wearing a T-shirt with his face painted on it. He would refuse to go to church, saying something about the theory of evolution. He used to talk to me in halting Korean when he was in a good mood, but now, when we get into an argument, he pushes me into a corner with his English, pointedly mixed with more difficult words. Finally I get angry and he grumbles that he can't get more than five minutes of conversation with me. As the days approached for him to leave for college, he would quietly sit next to me for a while and then go to his room.

The day we left the dormitory, after dropping him off, he seemed very small as he waved goodbye to our car. Now he is leaving us. I clenched my teeth. My wife complains that our son isn't enjoying college life, as he always answers our phone calls in his room. He likes books as my father did and felt guilty whenever I sent him money for tuition and expenses. Then he called my wife to boast of the job he got as a campus policeman and of the spending money he was earning.

The night the LA riots occurred, he called my store. "Dad, be careful." His voice over the phone sounded like "Daddy, I love you." My son's voice made me feel as if I were hearing my father's voice. At such times the image of my father superimposes itself over the face of my son. After the last spring break, he was about to get in the car to leave, but he turned instead to come over to me. Then he gave me a warm hug and left.

I feel my father in the movements of the poplar trees that I see outside my window in May. And I see the face of my father, the face in the picture. And I hear the wind rustling in the branches and become the faint chorus of my father, myself, and my son, cheering.

TRANSLATED BY KIM KYUN-NYUN AND STEFFEN F. RICHARDS

Jay Sang Rhee, a member of the Korean Center of the International P.E.N., has published three works: *Echo of San Francisco, Father and Son,* and *Poplar*.

SHORT STORIES

SHORT STORIES

Yong Ik Kim

The Wedding Shoes

BUT I COME again and again to watch the silk brocade shoes set on a crate before the old man at the market. My previous decision not to come any more made me stand longer each time at the market corner. Each day I returned, one more pair of wedding shoes was missing; no one seemed ever to look. Those buyers must have come like my memory of a wedding day that was not meant to be sad but was sad. Now on that wooden crate there remained only five pairs. As I peeked at the shoes until the white insides became lost in the shadow, they seemed to contain the whole emptiness of the refugee-crowded market. I would have emptied my moneybag for a single pair before they all went away, but I was still afraid I might buy sorrow instead of wedding shoes.

Between the late-autumn vegetable mongers and a fortune-teller who talked to lonely, superstitious faces, sat the shoemaker. On the day I first had discovered the old man in the market, I had been looking for new rice, the round full kernels, when suddenly I saw him. I went closer but stopped as soon as I recognized him—the shoemaker who had lived one fence behind my home before I came to Pusan. It was obvious he had fled from the war area, perhaps with the shoes on his back. My mind shrank immediately, and bitter poured out. I repeated aloud the old spiteful words, "Even a three-village fire does not hurt one when he imagines the burning of three year-old bedbugs that gnawed him."

How often my fists had closed tight, holding bitterness and sadness when I thought about that shoemaker—that mouth that had refused my proposal for his daughter in marriage and had even bragged about his trade and insulted the butcher's trade of my family. I might have nodded to the shoemaker's wife. Not to the old shoemaker. Never!

SURFACING SADNESS

That day when I had gone over to his home to open the marriage talk remained always closer to me than yesterday. It always cast a clear shadow before me as if I watched a mirrored picture in the river. No matter where I went, that picture always walked ahead. It was the day after an unexpected storm. The air was clear and rich leaving dreamy blue distance between the four hills and the sky. The thatched roofs of the village glistened young and smooth, for the farmers had recovered the wrinkled faces of their roofs with golden rice straw. Early, before the noisy sparrows that nested under our eaves could have flown to the harvest field, my father had left for the Pusan market to buy a beef cow. That morning, several farmers had come to our home saying they would need ribs of beef, veal, head parts of cow for their children's wedding parties. I had heard their lighthearted voices rolling on loud as if they were talking to someone across the fields. Each praised the match and home choice for his son or daughter, mentioning every pleasing thing that might have come from the lips of the matchmaker.

"Grasshopper mating time follows ours, you know." An old farmer said. "The new rice and the pleasant chilliness pull two together under the one quilt. The wedding food will not spoil. The whole valley will come to the banquet, and then over the autumn, moonlit hills, they will go home singing, using their full-rounded stomachs as drums to tap on, blessing our brides and bride-grooms."

They talked on till wine time when the sun was halfway between the hills and the sky. Then, leaving, they noticed the large pumpkins on the shoemaker's roof beyond our fence and spoke in praise. "Those are so heavy the roof may fall in." Having had no new coating of straw for several years, the roof looked gray—dark and too flimsy to support the pumpkins.

One farmer said to another, "When we were as young as green pepper days, we thought we could not marry without the shoemaker's silk brocade shoes. Don't you think our children are smarter than we were? They laugh at such expensive customs and tell us to buy beef instead."

My home was quiet again. My mother said, "I wish they had not talked so loud." And, it was true, as often as the farmers came to our house and told of the ripening talks for their children, just so often the shoemaker came home drunk at night and kept half the village awake. I could see why he had grown bitter and hurt, for few visited him to place orders for shoes. I could remember in my own green pepper days, or even just several autumns ago, the farmers would go first to place their orders for wedding shoes. It was to the shoemaker they told everything the matchmakers had said, forgetting to leave until their tobacco ran out. Only afterward would they call over the fence to tell us how much beef they wanted. Later, the village women would go to the shoemaker's to ask who had ordered wedding shoes and about all the other things he had heard. For the shoemaker knew the inside and the outside of everything as his work concerned village social life.

My mother would draw out a long sigh, an envious sigh, as she awaited customers, and say, "The shoemaker's threshold is being worn out by the people's feet." But that was long ago. Each year fewer farmers visited even over the fence. Instead, they came to our house to tell of their marriages and to buy beef.

I do not know what made me decide that day to go courting. Perhaps it was the pleasantly chilly autumn wind through the red, dusky maple; perhaps it was the color of the sky; perhaps it was the echoes of my heart to others' marriage talks; perhaps every thread of that colorful day might have moved my long-timid feet toward that house.

It was so near that a village woman might point a stranger to my house by saying, "If you fell on the shoemaker's yard, your nose would hit the butcher's house." Whenever I thought about proposing, however, the shoemaker's house receded many hills beyond. So my mind had crossed many hills, many a year, but finally that afternoon it had reached close to its destination.

I did not expect the shoemaker's daughter to be at home, for I knew she had gone to work in the kitchen of a relative. The shoemaker was out, too, but his wife was taking stems off red peppers, and she greeted me at the porch. At first, I thought, I must talk of something else on the way to my heart. But I felt my throat had become narrower, and the words would not come out. Her hollow cheek as it faced the autumn sun held the sadness I had seen there whenever money lenders stood at her gateway. At last, I had to say that I did not come for the money they owed us. Then there was nothing else I could say.

After what seemed an eternity of embarrassment, I blurted out, "I want to marry your daughter!" I could not look at her. I heard her saying that she would consult her husband. Then I looked, stealthily. Her face clearly showed a pleased acceptance. I don't remember what else she said. When I left, I felt I had left my eyes behind, watching every expression on the happy face of the shoemaker's wife.

At home when I told my mother about my visit, she said confidently, "The shoemaker will be so glad to welcome a prospective son-in-law that the next time you visit him he may put both his legs into one leg of his wide trousers."

That night I could not sleep. I went in and out of my room many times to see whether the shoemaker had returned. Amid the fallen leaves in the frosty yard and the crickets, I waited for his footfalls that would presage the brightest moment of my life.

The stars glistened so close to the hills that the flying kites might be able to reach them, I thought. I could think of nothing that might prevent my marriage. If two cousins had been as friendly as the shoemaker's family and ours had been, they would have been called "closest cousins." The gourds that grew on the dividing fence were always shared without a quarrel. My father had been selling the shoemaker ox hide ever since I could remember. Of late, as he was very proud, his wife would come to us, asking that we sell her some hides and promising to pay the following month. We knew they would not pay, but we let her have one piece large enough for two pairs of shoes. So now, whenever his material ran out, the shoemaker would come home late at night, singing a happy song in the saddest of tones, and with his bitter, drunken remarks, awake the neighbors. His wife, by chance meeting my parents on the street, would hasten to bring up some startling piece of gossip, then hurry away. We knew she was trying to divert our minds, so we never mentioned money.

The shoemaker had always liked me. When I was not higher than the fence, he would make room for his daughter and me to sit in a corner of his workroom, putting aside his small adze, chisel, and nails. I was fascinated as I watched him stud the round silver nails in the hide bottoms, paste bright-colored silk on the up-turned sides, then put brocade of matching color on the nose of the shoes. He once said to me, "When you grow up to marry, I'll make the most beautiful wedding shoes for you, for your bride, and for the matchmaker."

Again one day, he looked at my face, then glanced at his daughter and called my name. "Sang Do, you have a clean, handsome face. Your matchmaker won't wear out her shoes, going to your future bride's home so often to ripen the marriage talk. But—the bride's parents want a matchmaker to talk for them. The silvery tongue pleases them, you know."

His eyes were lowered toward the shoes, but his mouth, slightly smiling, faced toward me. I felt the magic of his twisted mouth—the mouth that always opened to talk about brides, bridegrooms, their parents, and the go-between women. In those days he had made a living by making at least three pairs of shoes each month, one for each of the bridal couple and one for the matchmaker.

His daughter and I later went to school together across two hills. He let her wear silk brocade shoes, even to school. Often she did not want to wear them, for she was the only girl who did, and she could not run as fast as the other girls.

With his bamboo pipe in his mouth, holding out a pair of shoes toward me, he asked, "Sang Do, don't you think the sky blue silk and red brocade are beautiful? Don't you like my daughter more if she wears these shoes?"

I nodded to him, with honesty. I did not see any advantage in being born a girl except for one thing—to wear silk brocade shoes.

The village women talked about the Buddha mole between her eyebrows, the dimples in her cheek that would attract boys, but as far as I was concerned, I never thought about her face. I loved her shoes that others did not have. With them, to prevent chafing, she wore white muslin socks, and on the narrow path to the school, I often walked a step behind, watching the line between the white socks and the canoe-shaped shoes. The line always gave me the feeling that I was talking the sweetest nap, I would cross, carrying her on my back, using all my strength not to fall. She would cling to my back like a green frog, and how I loved those shoes dangling on either side on my waist.

As I advanced in the elementary grades, I seldom watched the shoemaker. The outdoors interested me more, and besides, he talked very little about weddings now. His mouth remained glued tight even when I asked whose shoes he was making. Somehow that twisted mouth looked unbearably bitter and unapproachable. I was surprised one day when it unfastened abruptly. "Nowadays," he said, "It is more like grasshoppers mating. Hasty marriages without putting on wedding shoes. It's workers' shoes, Western shoes, rubber shoes. I would rather have my daughter wear silk brocade shoes for one day than rubber shoes for a hundred days."

I then realized he was making shoes without orders for them. My eyes stared at the insteps, then I forgot what I was looking at. The unfinished shoe seemed to float away as it became larger until it looked like an ownerless boat on an uncharted sea. I could not understand why the farmers did not covet such a beautiful thing. As I watched the blood vessel swell in the shoemaker's neck, he continued, "They think they can buy three pairs of rubber shoes with the money they would pay for one of mine. But I would not trade one of mine for a hundred of theirs."

Young as I was, I knew he was getting poor. In autumn he did not even patch his roof, where it might leak the next summer. When his daughter came to buy beef with too little money, I very much hoped that my father would give her a generous amount. He always did. When in late summer the alarm of a coming typhoon startled us, the wife and daughter came to our home for an overnight stay, bringing with them a carefully wrapped bundle of silk brocade shoes. They feared their roof might blow off.

I did not realize, though, how hopeless the situation was until one spring day when his daughter told me that she would quit school and become a kitchen maid. I begged her to reconsider, promising that I would steal beef from my house to give to her if she would not leave, but that did not prevent her from going. She stayed at the Tile-Roofed House earning her three meals a day.

On my way home from school, I would walk by the house, but I could not go inside. I would stand on my toes and stretch my neck trying to see her through the space between the end of the house and the sorghum hedge. I was not tall enough, especially when the hard rains washed the road down as deep as a creek. Only when she came out could I get a glimpse of her—of her full skirt, her brocade shoes. How beautiful they were—the shoes which stayed longer in the air than they did on the ground. I felt as if the Tile-Roofed House were taking away my wedding shoes.

All that spring, while the green frogs sang in the rice field, I went every day to see the moving shoes. Soon, however, the double-chinned farmer of the house found me peeping into his yard, and he planted a cherry tree to fill the space where I had stood. Word got around as quickly as the light of the kerosene lamps after sunset in the village homes, and every man smiled at me without saying a word. Vehemently, the shoemaker said to me, "Sang Do, I won't lower the price. I'll let her wear them even in other people's kitchen, and when she marries, I'll let her take all the shoes with her."

The wedding day he mentioned seemed remote, far beyond many mountains. I thought with despair how many straw shoes I would have to wear out to reach my wedding day. The

SURFACING SADNESS

shoemaker raised my chin with his stubby thumb, and, looking into my eyes hopefully, said, "Perhaps next autumn, some wedding homes will buy shoes. Then she will be able to return"

Since that spring the cherry tree had borne ripe round fruit five times. Still she did not come back but worked on in another family's kitchen. And now, on the night after I had made my marriage talk, I decided that before the snow came I would take a big ox hide to the shoemaker for him to make the most beautiful shoes for his daughter. On the wedding day, my home would spread the white homespun linen for the shoes to walk on, as some do in a marriage between one-fence neighbors, instead of hiring sedan chairs.

The autumn night had deepened with the stillness, and I had walked I do not know how many times around the freezing yard, before I heard the hoarse, drunken voice of the shoemaker. He was putting his own words to a popular tune: "A farmer greeted me: It is a fine autumn day; how are your pumpkins growing, shoemaker?"

Soon a light brightened the square paper window, and a shadow moved across it. The shoemaker's wife had gotten up, I thought, to meet her husband. I shivered a bit. I went out and leaned over the fence, pressing my chest against it to listen to the wedding talk she would surely bring to him. In my impatience, I walked back a few steps, then back and forth to lean on the fence. At last I heard quarreling voices. The paper window was flung open as if by wind and the angry words flew out. "I won't give my daughter to a butcher's home."

I could not trust my ears to believe until I heard further. "Because I owe money to you butchers, did you think you could get my daughter as easily as a widower takes a servant girl? Butchers would not know that there is a matchmaker. She is the daughter of the finest silk brocade shoemaker within ten mountains."

The words came to me like round flower bowls falling one on another. His wife said something frantically, but her voice was drowned out by his cracking tones. The window was closed swiftly, his voice, however, being still loud enough for me to hear, as he said, "The flattering that comes under the tongue to get more pieces of beef has made the butcher's mind big. I am the wedding shoemaker!"

The next thing I remember is my mother standing beside me gripping my wrist and gasping. "What are you trying to do?" I found myself trembling at the gateway holding a butcher knife in my hand.

My mother snatched the knife away from me. I did not expect such strength from her. The tone of her voice was surprisingly severe. "You should not scratch others even with your fingernail. What would the people think of us butchers?"

Something clawed my inside and flattened my chest and stomach. I bit my own arm to forget that deep agony, but that did not lessen it. Then I knew it was pain that neither tomorrow nor the next day could ease. I slapped the earth and cried.

For many days I stayed in my room and avoided the sunshine as might an unmarried girl who was pregnant. When the sun was as low as the hill, I would walk up the nearest rise and bury my face in the golden foxtails and wonder how I was not crushed by such a mountain of sorrow.

Many people crossed the hill. Old women's feet looked heavier than others, some in soiled gray ox-hide shoes. The sight of the shapeless shoes sickened me. I did not notice at first that they had once been silk brocade ones. They moved as heavily as my heart.

The autumn crossed the hills and went farther. Not even in the brightest field, nor on the four hills, could I see autumn. One day when no one would be surprised if snow came, I saw the matchmaker go into the shoemaker's house. My heart was past sinking lower. One thing, however, I feared I could not endure to see was that the shoemaker's wife came to buy beef for her daughter's wedding and perhaps ask for a piece of hide for the shoes.

SURFACING SADNESS

My mother knew all the anxiety of my soul, and my father knew half. He arranged to send me to the Pusan butcher market, where I was to work with my uncle. My parents hoped that outside the valley I would become calm and change my directions with the wind, and tried to tell me that there were girls everywhere. My father did not say these things to me directly, but when I left for Pusan—a short winter's day walking distance—he said with provocative vagueness, "Chase the spring wind with city girls. Then your mind won't be fixed on one girl."

Spring did come to Pusan, after winter, with soft peppery winds from the Japan Sea. It blew the skirts of the city girls in every direction—but I did not chase the spring wind with city girls. Somehow my mind was always chasing the wedding shoes—the beautiful ones my childhood had dreamed of when I has watched in the shoemaker' workroom. Strangely, I did not picture the future bride, who now belonged to the past. She and her shoes never faced me. I was always behind her, watching the backs of the silk brocade shoes and white muslin socks with a canoe-shaped line around her feet. Whenever my mind followed, they crossed hill after hill as if destined to move away from me.

I could not stop chasing the wedding shoes until one day the war came to Pusan. My parents fled from their valley home and came to the city to live with me. People poured into the city. With no invitation, they were guests of no house, but guests of the dusty street. Road guests, they called themselves. As they could not, of course, feed their oxen, they sold them to the butchers for a dog's price. The paper money of inflation piled up in my pockets like leaves, without adding to my joy. It did not even occur to me that I was thinking about the brocade shoes any longer.

Summer passed, leaving no memory behind. I did not notice autumn until it had almost gone. Somewhere within me, the fleeting shadow of southward birds moved over the cropped fields. I wondered in the market, vaguely looking for new rice. Suddenly, my eyes fell on the wooden crate with the silk brocade shoes upon it. The nose of the shoes faced me, watching. I do not know why I went closer—only to fill my mind again with anger and bitterness. My impulse was to take all the shoes and fill them with money to show my wealth, but four or five steps before the crate, I stopped. So many wrinkles had gathered in the face of the shoemaker that his twisted mouth looked like a tallowless wick. That mouth would not open any more to brag. I stayed to see who would buy his shoes. No one even looked at them, except the market hangers-on who asked the price of everything. One of them shouted, "Charging sky-high prices for behind-the-time shoes! Old man, you are asleep, scratching another's leg instead of your own itching one."

He remained sitting with unbending back, unmindful of their taunts. The front of his stomach looked as if it had touched his back.

As his piles of shoes began to diminish, I came again and again to look. The hard feeling against him was receding farther and farther as his wares dwindled. Instead, sadness rose in me and rose again. As the days grew cold, the twisted mouth opened to draw out coughs without white breath. I wondered what would become of him when all his shoes were sold. In my mind, the coughing mouth would blur into one that had once been opened with smiles over his own wedding talks in his own warm workroom. How light the wedding shoes looked, I would think.

Then I would grow aware of the noises of the market and walk with the crowd: every kind of shoes—straw shoes, and hobnailed shoes. All looked so heavy. It might be that the weight was determined by the wearers. There was nothing joyful left in this land, not even one day of joy, the joy that would fill the mouth of the wedding shoes.

Sometimes I hoped he would recognize me. Then I would have a chance to ask him what had become of his wife and daughter. He did not notice me, however. At least, there never was a sign of recognition in his unblinking eyes, and I could not speak first. I did want to possess a pair of his shoes before all went to strangers. But I was afraid I might buy wedding shoes that were not wedding shoes. I watched his merchandise with the intensity of one who sees a night road ahead just before the moon hides behind the black clouds.

When I saw only three pairs left, I did not come any more. It was unbearable to watch the shoes whose brocade noses faced me and knew they would soon go away, leaving the memory of their backs.

The first snow came early. The footsteps on the road touched me as if the silk brocaded shoes had gone that way, the finest silk getting wet. Then I realized that the snow could actually be wetting the silk. I hurried back to the market, hoping the shoemaker had not brought his shoes this afternoon and at the same time hoping he had. I could hear my heart beat as I came near the market corner. Two pairs on the crate under a black umbrella faced me. I was glad, holding a joy in my two fists as tight as possible.

I did not see the shoemaker. Someone else was there—a yellow blanket over her drooping shoulders and her dark hair fluffed with snow. She was holding the umbrella over the shoes, rather than over herself. Was she the wife of the shoemaker? At first I was not sure; she had so greatly changed. But later, I knew it was she. The snow was falling slantwise. I wished she had wrapped the shoes and taken them home. I did not know why she did not.

A man wearing a Western style coat and wide Korean trousers stopped and looked through his eyeglasses as he spoke to the old woman. As he was fishing in his pocket, I walked up, taking all the money I could hold in my hand, and putting it down in front of her, I said, "Here—let me buy the shoes."

The man was perhaps the one who ran an antique shop or sold souvenirs. He gave me an unhappy look. His anger might have been visible had it not been for the fluffs of snow that misted his glasses. He left, talking to himself.

She dropped the yellow blanket and pulled her head back as if my money were counterfeit and I was trying to deceive an old woman. Her gray eyes were tired, sorrowfully indifferent, like the wintry road that could not hold more shadows. I hastened to say, "I am Sang Do. Where is your husband?"

For a moment she looked at me absently, then her lips quivered violently and showed her toothless gums. I heard her crying without voice, a hoarse sound like the winter wind. I knew then a hopeless thing had happened, for I had seen the same manner of crying from old woman who had lost their dear ones. I picked up the umbrella she had dropped and held it over the shoes. The flakes of snow fell at the line of the shoes. The old woman took each shoe reverently, wiped the snow from it, then placed it on a newspaper with one over the other and wrapped them carefully.

"He did not want to sell them to strangers," she said, "at rubber-shoe price. But I chased him out from the refugee quarters every morning. He would lower the price on just one pair for two or three days. Then I nagged him again to sell. When only two pairs were left, he was stubborn as a child. He would come out to the market, but always came back with two pairs—until—the cold, empty stomach…"

She did not finish her words. I did not know whether it was the snow or something else that ran down her cheeks. Then with sudden ease, she resumed. "He died in front of the silk brocade shoes. I know that was all he wanted."

She looked for a moment at the paper money I had put down on the crate, then handed the wrapped parcel to me as she added, "With this money, I can give him a decent burial."

I did not take the parcel. I felt as if I would be taking it from the shoemaker's hand that still held it as tightly as a sleeping child holding a willow whistle. I shook my head and said, "Keep the shoes for your daughter."

For a moment, I wondered whether her daughter had married. Then I realized it no longer mattered. She was now the owner of the silk brocade shoes. I just wished she would be alive somewhere to receive them. I folded the yellow blanket, pushed the money inside, and put it over the bundle of shoes. When I had placed them in the arms of the old woman, she held them all closely for a moment, then walked out bending her head slightly as if carrying a baby.

"My daughter," she said, "is dead. She was killed last summer in the bombardment."

Ah, but I already knew. I had already felt this death in my heart. Opening the umbrella, I followed her a few steps behind, stretching my arm forward to shelter her. Someone behind us shouted, "There is a good place. Someone is moving out, leaving a wooden crate!"

Outside the market, the wind blew up snow. I adjusted the umbrella to a half-open position so that the wind would not grab it away and followed, hoping she would not fall with silk brocade shoes.

Yong Ik Kim was known as an outstanding short story writer in the US, Europe and Korea. He published his short stories in the *New Yorker* and the *Atlantic*. His novels were published by Little, Brown, Alfred Knopf and Double Day. He received his master's degree from University of Kentucky, and taught creative writing courses at Duquesne University in Pittsburgh. His novel, *The Happy Days*, was selected as an outstanding juvenile book of 1960 by the *New York Times*. "From below the Bridge" and "Village Wine" were cited as outstanding short stories in Marther Foley's *Best American Short Stories* in 1958 and 1976, respectively. "The Wedding Shoes," his debut short story in the United States, first appeared in the *Harper's Bazaar* in 1956.

Before his death in 1995, Yong Ik Kim had designated Mrs. Faith M. Leigh to be his literary heir, and she has graciously given her permission to reprint "The Wedding Shoes" in this volume.

Sang Ok Song

Echo

IT WAS LATE November when he called me from New York. He said that he was going to visit Korea passing through Los Angeles, and that he wanted to see me on his way. Because he had no other reason to stop at Los Angeles, if I was not available, he could go to Seoul straight from New York. As he said there was no burning necessity, it seemed that he just wanted to see me. Since I thought of him from time to time and was wondering how he was doing, I wanted to see him, too. Besides, I had no plan to go someplace else, and there was no reason to keep me from seeing him.

One thing I was wondering was what on earth made him want to go visit the homeland. When I met him long time ago in New York, for whatever psychological motive it was, he didn't hesitate to say that he had no particular reason to go to Korea—not many thoughts of it came to his mind—and that he didn't want to go to the country. His attitude was so firm that I couldn't even ask him why.

Youngsoo Kim. I got to know him twenty some years ago. Of course, it was in Seoul. He and I were both new college graduates, then. We lived in the same boardinghouse near a college in Seoul for a while. Because both of us were from province, we had to live in a boardinghouse for sometime even after we found jobs.

We sometimes mingled with other fellow boarders in the neighborhood. I often went to a mountain with him, along with a few others. It was a mountain near Seoul. He was so sincere and positive on everything that he always volunteered to prepare food and drinks, and led us through new trails he found in the mountain.

Once on the mountain top, he would cup his hands around his mouth and shout out loud. His voice sent to the distant mountains and to the sky soon echoed back to him. He used to call it the voice calling himself. He was a lover of literature. He read almost all the poems and stories in literary magazines.

"The present-day poems, I don't understand no matter how hard I try. But as for the stories, I can see the efforts to express the pain of our time." In the early sixties, the politics and the society were drawn into a whirlpool, and people had to worry about the world in addition to their own personal problems.

He often told me his impressions after reading my works. "I think it takes a great courage to unfold one's own thoughts to the whole world. And it is also surprising that words can describe things so beautifully."

Our relationship didn't continue for long. At most two years, according to my memory. He left for America to continue his education. It was only for the first few months we wrote to each other. Then we stopped writing, and there was no more interchange between us. The relationship started in our transient period in a boardinghouse, and as it was short, we almost forgot about each other soon after we parted. His news came to my ear now and then. It was something like this if I summarize.

He completed his education to become a CPA as planned and opened an office in New York. He acquired qualifications of designated office from the government and other public organizations. Naturally, it brought more work and more money followed. According to a friend of mine, he enjoyed the status of an eastern establishment and the life of the American upper-middle class. I am not sure if the fellow exaggerated, but it seemed true that he had "succeeded" in America.

I just thought it was very likely so, as I remembered how sincere and positive he used to be. But the thought of him didn't stay in my mind for long. I didn't think I would have a chance to see him again in my life.

But the chance came to me. It happened ten years after he left the country, in other words about ten years ago from now, when

I still lived in Korea. On my trip to Europe and America, I stopped in New York. A friend of mine who learned of my travel plans gave me his phone number and suggested that I should call him.

He showed up at my hotel, looking exactly the same as ten years before. It was quite amazing; he didn't change a bit after so many years—probably so many years of hardship—in a foreign country. The only difference was that he seemed to have lost the spirited energy of his twenties and looked calm and a little tired. He also said I didn't change a bit.

He seemed to have been busy that day and told me he had spent the day in Washington, D.C. It was a warm day in early June. The sun was still up when we finished dinner at a Korean restaurant.

"It's a shame I don't have enough time to take you for sightseeing." That was what he said. I arrived in the morning and had to leave the next day. I just visited the Metropolitan Museum of Art and the Statue of Liberty by myself during the day. We drove around a few famous places in downtown New York. I think we spent about two hours in his car. During the time he repeatedly emphasized how pleasant and satisfactory his American life was.

"Isn't New York the capital of the world? It's the center of everything. Everything starts here and ends here. Forget about everything else. Isn't it a great privilege to be able to sit here and watch world-class performing arts?"

It was then that he said he had no particular reason to go to Korea, not many thoughts of it came to his mind, and that he didn't want to go to the country. Until then, since he had left Korea some ten years before, he said he'd been to Korea just once, about six or seven years back.

He said he went to get his parents. After his parents came to America, the one last string to the country seemed cut off. The homeland to him was not more than an old sack of not-so-meaningful memories. He thought he could throw it into a river if he had to. "My parents often go and visit the homeland. I am very happy to see them enjoy it."

When he took me back to my hotel, he added a few more words as if he had just remembered. "Do you still write? It was fun reading back then. Why, I can't read any Korean books these days."

The next morning, I took a taxi to the airport. Youngsoo said he was busy but wanted to send one of his employees to help me, but I stopped him. It was not necessary, fifteen dollars could take me to the airport comfortably.

We met so briefly and that was it. We didn't have any occasion to write, nor did we try to keep in touch with each other in any other way. It had been already five years since I came to Los Angeles, and it was entirely due to my laziness that I did not let him know about it. It was only an excuse that I did not have his numbers. I could get it easily by asking around a few friends in New York.

But Youngsoo Kim was not the only person I knew. How can I keep in touch with everybody I know? So we'd been living like strangers though we both lived in America until he called me out of the blue and told me he wanted to see me.

He stayed in Los Angeles for a day. He arrived in the afternoon and left for Korea the next afternoon. We had dinner and spent only a couple of hours together. Our meeting was as short as when we met in New York ten years before.

And just like then, it was he who talked most and I again was the listener. His appearance had not changed much, but the white hairs here and there revealed his age. Speaking of the age, he was already getting close to fifty.

We exchanged usual greetings and asked each other how things were going on, but neither of us said we should have called earlier or anything like that. He said he heard from another friend that I was living in America.

He didn't answer me right away when I asked him if he had anything special to do in Korea during the visit. He just said he managed to find some time for vacation around Thanksgiving holiday.

When I asked, he said it had been three years since his last visit. He said that, two years before that, that is, five years before, his whole family visited Korea. I was somewhat surprised. So, he had made two visits since he told me he had no reason and no desire to go to Korea.

He began to talk as if he were reading my mind.

He didn't remember exactly when he began to think about showing his homeland to his children. The thought came to him one day like a bird flapping the wings, and it wouldn't leave his mind. He didn't know why it occurred to him and didn't try to find out. The thought that was obscure in the beginning turned into a must as time went by.

But it was not easy to find time for it. Then, something happened to his wife's family. If it had been before, he would have sent his wife alone. But he went along this time. He also took his two children with him. One was in elementary school and the other in junior high, but both were in their summer break.

There couldn't be a special meaning in taking the children to his homeland. But it was only for them that he took the time in their busy schedule to visit his hometown. He wanted to show his children his hometown, the place he grew up. His grandfather and grandmother's graves were also there.

During the two days he stayed in his hometown, he visited the school he went. Because he went to school before they reformed the educational system, his junior high and high schools used the same building.

The old school building he last saw in twenty-five or twenty-six years left him a strong impression. It stayed in his mind for a long time.

He went to junior high during the war and finished high school in the ruins of the war (It was same for me). It was especially bad because his hometown was in one of the regions that experienced direct damage from the war.

SURFACING SADNESS

Through his six years of junior high and high school education, it was only one year, his senior high-school year, that he could study in the original school building. For the other five years, he studied outside, moving from one place to another, or in some military tent, with wind fluttering around.

It was after a long time that he got a temporary school building built with boards in a corner of the playground. The original school building, where he should be studying, was being used as a military facility. The school and the backyard on the other side of the barbed-wire fence were a forbidden area. They were never allowed to enter. Sometimes, merely casting a glance was a scary thing. The place was filled with wounded soldiers.

After a quarter of a century, the school building did not change much but looked as old and shabby as before. Besides, it looked shrunken small along with the playground as small as a palm. How large the playground was, and how big the school building looked back then!

Only one teacher remained. Mr. Kim, who used to teach algebra, became an old man and was now the principal.

"Although the children nowadays are studying in an environment incomparably better than in our time..."

He said that many good students still have to give up college because of their family's financial problem. When he was in school, only a few students in each class went to college. He himself was in a condition far from being favorable. Not just because he remembered his difficult college years, but he couldn't help thinking there must be a way to help such students... He couldn't erase that thought even after he returned to the States, two years after that. So three years ago, he went back to his hometown again, this time by himself, for these reasons.

He still couldn't come up with a concrete plan. But the thoughts changed his view and the homeland now took on a different appearance for him.

The homeland that used to be only an old sac of not-so-meaningful memories, which he thought he could throw into a river if he had to, was now making keen touches on him.

He often dreamed of going to the mountain. It was the mountain he used to go when he lived in Seoul. And as he did then, he shouted out loud with his two hands cupped around his mouth. The voice he sent to the far mountains and the sky echoed back to him. It was his voice calling himself.

"I know it sounds strange, but whenever I thought of Korea, I remembered that time. I eagerly read the stories and poems, and it always brought you to my mind."

His visit to the homeland this time was to set up an educational fund for his hometown high school. He had to spend so much time in order to hammer out all the details. So, he called himself a slug.

"It took me five years time if I count from when I took my children there."

He said he was taking only a little amount of educational fund this time, but he was planning to send some more every year. He said that was the only way, as he was not a very rich person, but he also said he would try to maintain certain level to support at least a few students for their college tuition and other educational expenses.

I was pleased to witness not only a laudable anecdote but also a person's will to bring himself to maturity. Although my schedule was very tight as usual, I took him to the airport.

"I'll call you when I come back. I should give you a report." He smiled radiantly.

SURFACING SADNESS

TRANSLATED BY ELSIE HYERYUNG KIM

Sang Ok Song founded the Korean Literary Society of America in 1982, and is currently serving as its president. Besides being the recipient of many literary awards, Song has published a number of works, including the novels *Fantasy Murder, River of Darkness,* and *Buffalo Hunting*; story collections, *Black Christ, Season of Nightmares*, and *Floating Heart*; and a collection of contes, *Saturday, Nothing Happened.*

SHORT STORIES

Young K. Hahn

Guest

"DON'T BE TOO impatient. Time is not made up of just the future. I am not saying that I will tie you up leisurely." As soon as I walked into the hospital room, grandfather said these words. He was writing something down on the paper. It seemed that he had written several pages already. The upper part of the bed was nearly perpendicular to the floor. To avoid slipping off, his knees were supported as well. It was an awkward posture. He looked uncomfortable with a plastic oxygen tube going through his nose. The hissing sound of the oxygen tank was accentuated by the beeping noise of the IV pump. Glucose mixed with morphine, having passed through the pump, flowed through grandfather's veins.

He was working on the patient's table pulled close to his chest. As I tried to go near, he waved off with his hand. "Sit over there. I might need your help later, but…" I sat on a chair close to the entrance and waited for grandfather to finish his task. He had been working on the task for several days. While working on his writing, he would not let anyone come near him. In reality, the writing was rather predictable. We all knew what comprised his life. Even if he was writing his last will, there wouldn't be anything unusual about it. As far as I knew, grandfather was a petty farmer; as far as my father knew, before grandfather became a farmer, he had been an ambitious foreign student.

He was very thin. Although he had liver cancer, that was a mere excuse to wrap up the end of a body, with a stormy history, destiny. His body was passing his era. Other than his mental spirit, there was not one part of him that was not worn out. Grandfather's mental faculty was quite different from that of others.

It was even different from that of father's. It wasn't a fierce dream to achieve a certain goal, nor was it energy to retain a certain condition. It was in a vague form, yet it never let grandfather go, consuming his entire life. I had always felt that grandfather was tied to an unseen cord which made him go around his life in a wide circle.

When grandfather was done writing, unlike other days, he took all the paper into one pile and folded it into three sections. He stuffed it into an envelope and licked the flap to seal it. The movement looked slow and difficult. I wanted to help him. He again waved off his hand. He finished off the task, which he took a week by writing one line on the outside of the envelope. "Please carry out. Father." "Give this to ae-bee."

The man grandfather called ae-bee was my father who came constantly to this hospital room. I couldn't figure out why he called me to carry out this errand. But what could you do? The elders had formed something like rituals for every action through their lives. The rituals could be called worships. Even up to her death two years before, my grandmother had nagged me nearly everyday for eating with my left hand. Father was the same when it came to rituals.

After he handed over the envelope to me, he asked his head of the bed to be lowered. As if the several days' work had taken its toll, grandfather looked extremely tired. I adjusted the bed with slight incline near the head. Grandfather began to speak after modulating his breathing for a while: "For a farmer, water is always a worrisome factor. The quantity and quality of water. Constant worry about water has led me to think about something. Far away where I can't see, there flows a large river. Water from that river flows to my farmland. Water comes in and wets my land and then flows out toward that far away large river. Now, the river water is not the same as before. The earth, wind, and sunlight from my farm have mixed into the river. The river continues to flow, wetting the land below it. The water that has wetted the land continues to flow to the land below it. Don't blame your father too much. It is also the work of that far away river."

My father was working toward gathering all our relatives to New York. Like Flushing, where many Koreans live near each other like in an ant tunnel. He convinced my aunt, his sister, to move from San Francisco, where her family operated a supermarket, right after the Los Angeles riot. He insisted on hospitalizing my grandfather, who lived in Long Island, at the hospital with which he was affiliated. Now that I was nearing graduation from college, he was persuading me to follow his footsteps by entering a medical school. He hoped that I would work side by side with him in the future in the hospital he was currently planning to build.

His surroundings were quite lonely but I believed he found comfort in living close together. How much warmth would be generated from reflected heat from a small number of family members and what sort of shield could they form! At times, I found this all unbearable. If possible, I would like to live out in the space. Neither Korea nor America. Neither past nor present. A place that belonged to neither grandfather nor father—just mine. If only that was possible for me… The three often talked about aspects of life—work, leisure, and love—out of these, I never had the opportunity to possess even one myself.

Father was always a soldier at a war of survival. He knew his family as trusted allies, especially I, who was without a doubt his staff officer and a scout. Naturally father planned my tasks and any leisure activities were limited as much as possible. Love, well, unless it was potentially like a Korean woman, could be impossible. Suu Kyi was Myanmar 1.5 generation woman. She was from the country formally known as Burma.

Before I met Suu Kyi, I had only read about Aung San Suu Kyi once in a while in the newspapers. Other than that I didn't know much about Myanmar. The name of the country itself seemed somewhat uncivilized. However, after the country was overtaken by military dictatorship in 1962, children like Suu Kyi were born to change the era. Suu Kyi was called Suu Kyi because of Aung San Suu Kyi who is respected by all the people of her country. For the only child, naming her Suu Kyi was all her parents could do for her.

I met Suu Kyi last spring. While I was walking on the Washington Square, she stopped me and asked whether I could assist her with her photography. Nearby there was a demonstration underway with banners fluttering in the breeze. "More World, Less Bank!" "Fair Trade!" "Build the World Against Imperialism!" It was rather customary for demonstrations to occur when the United Nations had a major meeting.

I told her fine. She said that she would like to take a picture of my back and told me to walk casually toward where the banners were lined. I thought it was quite amusing. She thought I was a part of the demonstrators. Did the scale of my worry look like the world? As I turned and walked away, I was grinning self-consciously in light of the situation. Since it was the back, my face wouldn't be seen any way. After taking the picture, she handed me a card and disappeared through the crowd. The card in my hand was an invitation to Fashion Institute of Technology students' photography exhibit.

A month later, I sought out the photography exhibit opening reception to see how the fabricated association of the anti-globalization demonstration and myself became an art. Although I took a look around the exhibit, I couldn't find a photograph of me. After looking around thoroughly for a couple of times and not finding any, I became somewhat angry.

With a little more snooping around, I found Suu Kyi near the entrance of the exhibit, laying out refreshments. Would she recognize me? I went toward her and blocked her view. Surprisingly, she recognized me right away. After the recognition, however, she was glaring at me. She lifted out her backpack from the top of the soda box under the table. She took out several pictures and waved them before my face and spoke. "Here, take some free photographs. Are you happy now that you have wasted a poor student's time and effort and the cost of film?"

I looked over the pictures. I was smiling as I walked toward the fluttering "More World, Less Bank" banner. Even though it was the back of my head, I could still see the smile. It was obvious the association was fabricated. It made one think that the anti-globalization movement might have been created to curtail fabricated, international organizations, such as that picture. I was startled and amazed by the truth portrayed by the picture. I still had to apologize. Although I did apologize, her anger did not subside easily. I was finally out of debt after buying her a roll of film and promising that I would help her in the dark room a few times. A photograph is a shrewd animal.

I fell into photography while visiting her dark room. We tried several different experiments. No matter how we made up and covered it, the photograph showed how the subject reflected its life on earth. And amazingly, in that accumulated time of the past, the moment when the shutter went off also overlapped. It was three dimensional enough to detect smile from the back of the head. Further, the reverse image, teasingly created by a mirror, was corrected perfectly by the photography. It seemed that a photograph was closer to the truth than anything else.

I wanted to do photography. I had consumed all my time in the past year trying to persuade my father. However, there wasn't much time left. With graduation, Suu Kyi would be traveling to third-world countries, including Myanmar, to take pictures and I had decided to go with her. We were planning to travel the world and work as freelancers. I wanted to record the truth, not of Korea or America, but of the world, into a book. Neither grandfather nor father, neither past nor present, only the earth, wind, and sunlight of the future, I wanted it to be my land and my space.

Since I was raised into many molds, I couldn't bear that task alone. Right now, I needed someone like Suu Kyi, who would walk a step ahead of me. I really couldn't wait any longer. I really wanted to leave. Even though the effort of trying to persuade father was a stressful work. I couldn't leave my father in happiness now that persuasion had failed. I knew anyone with Korean blood couldn't do it. Ultimately, no matter what ways I lived—his or mine—I was doomed to suffer. Unless some dramatic change occurred, I was destined to consume my life going back and forth like pendulum between the two worlds.

It didn't seem likely that father would give up his task of bringing the family together, which he saw as his mission. Grandmother has passed away. When grandfather passed away, there would be four of aunt's family and three of ours left. Even if all the family members got together, as a third generation Korean family, it would barely be the size of a Jewish or an African-American family. They must have realized that part of the immigrant life that, after the worries of feeding and the freedom, there was a swamp of loneliness to be dealt with. Father didn't seem to realize that I could not resolve the responsibility of caring for loneliness. If it was at all possible, I would take the burden a hundred times over, but without any possibility, I could only feel the heavy weight of the burden. Even in a make-believe world, I didn't have that ability.

Father's anxiety and impatience were deeply rooted. Grandfather, who was a university student when the Korean War broke out, was falsely labeled as a good English speaker and ended up as an interpreter for an American officer. After the war, through that relationship, he was able to go to America as an ambitious foreign student. The fact that the expectations of the officer, who arranged his studies in America, and those of my grandfather were so different showed the actual English language proficiency of my grandfather.

Unlike his expectations, from the moment he landed in America, he had difficulty sustaining even himself. There was no one to blame. He was far away from Korea where any family, even with moderate means, would have provided room and board to a guest. My father was barely four and my aunt was two at the time.

Grandfather, who pledged to come back to Korea as a scholar, became a ranch laborer within three years of his arrival in America. He brought over his wife and children. The America which waited to nurture my father's childhood years was rural farm's naïve discrimination and territorialism. Discrimination came in many forms. It came as overt kindness and disrespectfulness. Overt kindness often turned abruptly to disrespectfulness. Grandmother often talked about that aspect.

There was a local plumber who took care of the town's drainage. He often called out "Mama San" whenever he saw grandmother. He was a Korean War veteran. She didn't like the name call. His countenance would suddenly change if she complained about how the drain clogged again since his last visit. He was still exchanging letters with the prostitutes he knew in Korea. In this manner, he was threatening in a subtle way that he could treat "Mama San" like those women. This infuriated grandmother. She implied that he knew the distinction between woman like her and the woman of the streets. Between the two classes, there lay a silver dagger. The dagger, which clearly divided the two classes of women, was an emergency suicide weapon. Even in America, grandmother carried the silver dagger with her.

Naturally, father grew up in loneliness and distress. Grandfather wasn't much of a help to his family's lives by working on his farm and living in seclusion. Although grand-mother said that grandfather had quit his education due to poverty, grandfather never agreed or disagreed to this statement.

Nonetheless, it was difficult to figure out why after three years of school, he quit his education and became a ranch laborer. As a changed person, he just silently cultivated the earth and detoured around the life around him. Therefore, it was father who had to stand before grandmother, who didn't even know the English alphabet. It was his younger sister who had to combat the world.

Father, not only for himself, but also for his family, had to put all his effort into academic studies, which he saw as a shield of protection. He couldn't think of any other defense mechanism. He didn't have any fellow Koreans he could hang out with or lean on to.

There weren't any clear events he would need to complain about to the authorities. They were too vague and mundane.

SURFACING SADNESS

Luckily, his unique survival method of hard work and effort gave him enough reward. He was the first graduate from a rural Long Island high school to be enrolled in an Ivy League college. He said that up until that day he couldn't be relieved from the anxiety of the battlefield. Father said that, in many aspects, it was much easier at the medical school.

Since he was on his back in silence, I thought grandfather was asleep. With his eyes closed, he began to speak to me. "A guest may be arriving. If he arrives after something happens to me, I hope you will take care of him. He is the same age as you."

"Who is it?"

"Even if the grown-ups don't take to liking him, I would like you to look after him. A foreign country is new to him... He wouldn't know much..." "Grandfather, who is it, really? Who's coming?" "His name is Jae-Seung." "But, that's your name."

Grandfather still had his eyes closed. His face was ashen. Was his conscience becoming blurry? Saying his name as that of the guest... Saying that a guest would be arriving... I was startled into fear. Was this what dying was about? I hesitantly got up to move toward his bed. The hissing noise still came from the oxygen tank. Maybe the morphine was being fed too fast? What shall I do? Should I call all? Grandfather suddenly opened his eyes wide. His ashen face was turning red.

"Jae-Seung will come ... Jae-Seung... If you could..." Grandfather coughed. Due to coughing, his speech was disconnected. And then he began to vomit something dark and crimson. With disjointed words, grandfather's remaining time was thrown up and out. I ran out to call the others. The doorbell rang. The tension could be gauged by how everyone's eyes became focused on the door. Even my adolescent cousins who, in their formal wears, were surreptitiously fooling around, stopped for a moment and restrained their movements.

Father was even more anxious because he hadn't made up his mind about his attitude. He tried so hard not to lose dignity as a responsible one for all the familial affairs. In his inside pocket, there was grandfather's envelope. I couldn't tell whether father had opened it or not. In any event, he was aware of my presence as the deliverer and glanced at me now and then.

I could understand why grandfather had deliberately asked me to deliver the letter. It was my father's and my task to untangle the contents together. It looked as if my mother and aunt had decided what their position would be. They were upset since our "guest" called yesterday morning. In any moment, there could have been temperamental outburst as a flaw in this solemn bidding of final farewell. Everyone was careful about what to say and what to do.

There were about two hours to go before the funeral service. The originally scheduled morning service was postponed to the afternoon due to the expected arrival of the 'guest.' Nonetheless, we had been waiting in our formal wear since this morning. I didn't think it would be necessary to be in a suit all day but decided to sit properly on a sofa so as not to get on grown-ups' nerves. Father's gaze hovered over me now and then. No one was willing to open the door readily. I got up slowly and moved to the foyer. Father followed hesitantly behind in a couple of steps. My aunt stood and uncharacteristically folded her arms. I slowly opened the door. My uncle walked in first as if he were unaffected by anything. That quality was both his strength and weakness. It was the reason he ended up being responsible for an important mission of going to the airport. Before starting out he had asked father. "How would I recognize him since there will be many people arriving from Korea?"

Father answered him cautiously. "His name is Jae-Seung…" As soon as it was heard, my mother and aunt let out "Oh, my God!" at the same time. Uncle gave a sudden loud laugh and spoke to his wife, my aunt. "Jae-Seung? Hey, mom, his name is Jae-Seung."

Father must have loved him considerably. Behind my uncle, the "guest" followed in. I was very surprised. Everyone else was surprised as well. My mother gave father once over. Thin and with a small build. An unnecessarily serious expression. Determined, very careful steps. He looked very much like my father.

It gave me an eerie feeling. There was someone else who resembled my father more than his son—me.

No one spoke; all were standing. On his way to the kitchen, uncle turned and impatiently shouted, "Mom, what are you doing? Shouldn't he be at least taking a shower so he could attend the funeral? He must be tired. Why don't you draw up his bath water?"

Father said, "Here, here," and ushered him into the living room, adjacent to the foyer, and sat him on the sofa. He sat my mother and aunt next to the "guest." My cousins were called in and asked to sit down.

"Your name is Jae-Seung?" Father asked. It was as if he could only believe it by verifying it again. "Yes," as if not to show timidity, the guest lowered his eyes and cut the answer short. The Nike vinyl bag, the one he had carried on his shoulders, was neatly placed on his lap. Smell of new vinyl, freshly out of mold, came from the Nike bag.

"Today is grandfather's funeral. Oh, before that, let me introduce the family to you." Father introduced the family members one by one. Without much response, he bowed his head lightly. He seemed to want to say that it really didn't matter. "When the funeral is over, I will be leaving; I won't be a burden to you," he seemed to say.

When father introduced me, I stuck my hand out. He hesitantly got up and grabbed my hand. I was quite surprised. His hand was very rough. It felt like grabbing grandfather's hand. Silence ensued with the end of the introductions. He had closed his mouth tightly and looked down upon his feet, without showing any emotion. Everyone was uncomfortable with loss for words.

Since the "guest" was living up to his title perfectly, mother and aunt's expressions became less rigid and they seemed to recuperate their emotional balance. I got up and guided him to the second floor. After leading him to the guestroom, I opened the bathroom door for his shower. He lightly pushed me out, as I was about to close the bathroom door for him. He went back to his room. He retrieved his Nike bag and went to the bathroom once again and closed the door.

Most of the guests at the funeral were the members of the church where my mother and aunt attended. Most of father's friends and colleagues from the hospital came to yesterday's viewing service. As today was a weekday, they couldn't attend. Suu Kyi, with her camera, made a beeline among the guests, quietly but quickly. Whenever my mother sensed the line Suu Kyi was making, mother's unfriendly gaze landed on me. I knew it meant "tell her to stop roaming around," but I ignored it. I took her to yesterday's viewing service and introduced her to the family.

Seemingly due to the state of things, except for mother and my cousins, no one else responded one way or another. Mother strongly disapproved, and my cousins couldn't suppress their curiosity and tried hard to find out more by looking back and forth from me to her.

Once this "guest" event got equalized, I was sure it would become quite an event. I was having absurd thoughts while watching her take pictures. When we developed these pictures later, we would really know who was truly grieving... which one would I be...

The "guest" seemed to have taken after my father. His movements were very disciplined, serious and cautious. Standing next to him, I could feel the strain he exerted in order to keep him from making mistakes. Whatever I did, within a few seconds, he instinctively followed. It seemed that there was no way to distinguish him from our family other than his sagging suit. When roses were thrown on the coffin, he and I were facing each other across the grave. Since there weren't any planned stations, father stood next to him. With the hymnal, the funeral was coming to an end. Someone tossed dirt onto the coffin. At that moment, I saw tears welling in his and father's eyes. From behind me, Suu Kyi's camera flashed. My own eyes were filled with tears after seeing theirs. Suu Kyi was missing out on taking picture of me at the moment. It would have taken her some time to go around the people. However, from behind my back, she didn't seem to even attempt at it. I must be once again just used for my back. At times like this, I had no doubt that Suu Kyi would be a successful photographer.

For Jae-Seung, this must have been a strange funeral. It was a funeral where he was endlessly mentioned by the name of the deceased. Finally, my curiosity was aroused. After grandfather passed away, the "guest" called from Korea to say that he was on his way. The entire family's attention was focused on him, but I was not interested in the details.

When father said that the "guest" was grandfather's grandson he somehow managed to have in Korea, it was enough information for me. It was not an unusual circumstance and I didn't think it warranted having the whole family's nervous tension at its peak. It was a very possible situation that could happen easily. It was amusing to see the grown-ups, who knew more about the situation prior to the "guest" existence, not being able to digest the information.

Just like grandfather, who seemed to have lived his life by trotting the circumference of it as if tied to something, they were also tied to something and was side stepping around the main circle of life. At any event, my curiosity was renewed to see how the earth, wind, and sunlight from grandfather's dark period would seep through Jae-Seung. From a common river called grandfather, just two generations down, it divided into tributaries. How had it changed in its flow? What were the grown-ups afraid of or unable to digest that they were on their nerves' edge?

Since there were many Korean guests, the dinner was reserved at a Korean restaurant. Mother and aunt were busy serving the preordered rice cakes and fruits. Having formally thanked the guests as a representative of the bereaved family, father urged Jae-Seung and I to hurry with the meal. We left early after asking uncle to manage the rest of the evening. I urged Suu Kyi, who wanted to take more pictures, to leave with us. After seeing her car leave, I hopped into father's car, whose engine he already had turned on.

Father drove silently. It was a long way. Even though it seemed there was no definite destination, father drove his car toward grandfather's farm, as if out of habit. The car sped pass through Manhattan toward the east. It took about two hours to arrive at the farm. Having avoided the evening rush hour, the car sped without much interruption. In the backseat, Jae-Seung looked out the window without a word. He must have been very tired but he didn't take his eyes off the window scene. There was glow in the sky as seen in the rearview mirror.

Upon remembering grandfather's charge, I felt bad about Jae-Seung. Be good to him, he had said. Even if the grown-ups disapproved of him, I was asked to be still kind…

"Jae-Seung!" When I called out, father in the driver's seat was startled first and looked at me. He probably thought I was calling out grandfather's name. It was still quiet in the back. When I turned around, he silently regarded me as if to ask what business I had with him. "What's your major?" Father revised my Korean and English mixed question accordingly so he could understand. "Rehabilitation medicine."

Father quickly turned around to look. Then he was attending a medical school? But he was supposed to be the same age as I was. Even if he just got into the medical school, he couldn't have selected his field of medicine yet.

I asked him again, "In Korea, do you decide which field before you start the medical school?"

Father explained that the Korean medical school system is different. As a freshman, one enters school of medicine and finishes it in six years. "Well, then, in two years you will be graduating. Lucky to be done with it early. Here, you have to be in school for eight years."

He responded quickly to my statement. "It is not a medical school. It's a two-year vocational education program." I couldn't fully understand. A kin of my father couldn't possibly be satisfied with health education school. It couldn't be from a lack of intelligence either. Besides, how could he be still in a two-year program? He should have graduated a while back.

I asked again, "You are still in school? Didn't you say it's a two-year program?" Although it was quiet behind me, the mood was strangely chilly.

After a while, I looked back. As if uncomfortable, father fiddled with the rearview mirror. He was trying to read Jae-Seung's expression through the mirror. I was startled when I looked back. The rim of his eyes was red. He was staring straight at me with those eyes. In confusion, I sat straight at first but didn't want to look as if I were disregarding his emotions. I turned back again. To me, who was flustered and at a loss for words, he too felt that he had to say something. His voice shook as he tried to subdue his emotions.

"Yes, it is a two-year program, but even after four years, I haven't graduated yet. After attending for one semester, I had to take a year off to earn tuition and a living. Even after that, if father ends up in a hospital from complications of alcoholism, I have to use that tuition money for the hospital fee. Did you know why I ended up choosing rehabilitative medicine?"

I didn't know what to say. Feeling like a criminal, I sat straight and looked out to the road ahead of us where the darkness was falling. Now there weren't any cars without headlights on. I felt impatient with the continuing fall of the darkness. I had to say something, but didn't have the slightest idea of what. If Suu Kyi were here, she would know how to overcome a situation like this, as if it were of no significance.

Not only I, but also father who felt the heaviness of the silence. Father quietly spoke, as if to say what was needed to be said. "How serious is your father's alcoholism? And I did hear from grandfather that there isn't anyone to look after him…" Jae-Seung's voice had settled low.

Talk of that kind showed that father had heard and known a lot more than I had thought from grandfather. "He cannot do any work and stay at home, so, he is really a disabled person. He used to work at a construction site but that was a long time ago. Right now, he spends more time at the hospital. He drinks and cries a lot. So it's sometimes unbearable. It's been worse lately, after grandfather paid us a visit in Korea."

"That must be two years ago when your grandfather went to Korea. How long has it been since your father saw grandfather's last?"

"Since he last saw him when he was two, it's really not seeing him at all. But I think there were correspondences up until my grandmother's death."

"I heard that your grandmother passed away early in the age. What did she die of?"

"I don't know."

"I am curious about one thing. I know it would be difficult, but please try to answer it without misunderstanding. How come that through all these years there wasn't any correspondence but now there is?"

Jae-Seung was quiet for a while. He seemed to be agonizing over how to understand or analyze this question.

He spoke up in a rather businesslike tone. "I wrote to grandfather. Father had always cherished grandfather's letters like treasures. I didn't really expect the letter to reach the receiver, what with the address from before my birth... I wrote a letter without much expectation, but a response came. And grandfather visited us. He said that he would come again, but..."

"Then up until two years ago, grandfather had no idea that he had another grandson in Korea?" Father and I both turned around to look at Jae-Seung. In place of an answer, he nodded and quickly turned his gaze to the window. The car must have crossed over a lane. A horn blared loudly form behind. Father quickly turned the steering wheel. All of us were tilted sharply to one side and then resumed the former position. It was unthinkable for this to have happened, while father was driving. I looked over at father, but he continued to look to the front of the road as if it weren't that important.

Father quietly drove. There was a part of father's question Jae-Seung didn't answer.

The person who could have helped his father, in other words, Jae-Seung avoided the part about his mother. Father didn't pursue the question. We arrived at the farm after the nightfall. Even though we called it a farm, if one saw the house as a whole, one couldn't tell whether it was a farm or not. Except for grandfather's lot, which was surrounded by tight grove of trees, there were houses all around. Grandfather had lived in this house for a long time.

Grandfather and grandmother used to argue a lot about possible disposal of this house. As far as I could remember, no part of this ranch style house was remodeled. After ending a long drive, we sat down on the chairs on the front porch. As always, the wooden chairs creaked. The house was pitch dark. Even father seemed to be reluctant to go into the dark house right away. Wasn't this the first time to see grandfather's house without a light on? Even in the middle of the night, grandfather had lit a small lamp by the window in the living room. As if to say that someone hadn't returned home yet. Jae-Seung leaned his head on to the back of the chair as if he were extremely tired.

I pulled out the key from the pottery used as an umbrella stand. The pottery was actually Korean *kimchi* urn, but, with a plastic liner in it, it was used as an umbrella stand. It was our long habit to place an emergency spare key underneath the plastic liner. Father turned on the small lamp by the living room window. Jae-Seung, who stood by the foyer, tiredly gazed at the warm light infusing from the lamp. I guided him to the upstairs bedrooms. When I told him to sleep in any room he wanted, he quietly went into grandfather's room.

Without the lights on, father and I sat across from each other at the dining room table. The table was placed by the window, with the view of the ranch. Due to the small size of the house, there wasn't a distinct partition between the dining room and the living room. Nonetheless, the light from the living room wasn't much of a disturbance.

While father looked out the farm through the window, I went into the kitchen, left to the living room, and put a kettle on to boil some water. As important as Jae-Seung was, I had to resolve my plans with father. The graduation was within a month.

With teacups before us, we were helpless for a while. We were deeply immersed in our own notions as we looked out the window. It was too dark to see the farm. The sky, which was dark and indigo like deep sea, kept a clear boundary with the dark earth. Was the far away river flowing into that dark and indigo sea? There was probably a lot of weed in the field where my grandfather had spent most of his life cultivating. It had been a long time since someone took care of it. I shall mow it down the next day. With the boundary of grandfather's land, which didn't seem large any more, the neighbors' lights were glittering at intervals. There were many extravagant homes around. It seemed to call for a change of use for this land by using some method.

Grandfather planted mostly greens and vegetables like many varieties of Chinese cabbage, radish, chives, sesame leaves, green onions, and other greens, which he sold to local Korean groceries. He distanced himself away from the earth, after grandmother passed away and he came back from a visit to Korea. He didn't even garden so as to while away time. Before he was taken ill, he was only busy getting himself ready to go out to Korea again. If he were still living and in good health, he would tell us that he had permanently returned to Korea, by now.

After finishing his tea, father turned on the light hanging from the ceiling above the table. The image of father and son was reflected on the window screen. The image was so unfamiliar that both of us turned away from it at the same time. After turning away from the window, father took out the envelope from his inside pocket. The envelope was still sealed. After opening it, father pushed the empty envelope toward me and started to read the letter, page by page. I looked over the envelope once again. "Please carry out. Father."

With that asking of favor left as homework, grandfather took leave of this world. The timing of the asking and the death seemed to be grandfather's plaintive will. As if to put a last weight to that asking of favor... Father meticulously read each page as if not to miss anything and afterward he handed the read pages to me in order.

When the war started, I was twenty-one years old. Since I got married on April of that year, I was still a newlywed. Fortunately, I was an interpreter for an American officer. I was better off than most people. As a matter of course in the war, I have seen many, many women who became helpless widows. One day, I was riding on a jeep when we heard the sound of a bomber. After parking the car under a tree, we ran into a nearby building. It was hard to say we were living creatures, but, at that period of time, the determination to live enabled us to be very much alive and active. However, there was a young woman who stood in the middle of the road, dazed out. People yelled at her to hide. She didn't understand, as if shocked by terror. She kept asking "What? What?" as she turned around in a circle. It seemed that she couldn't take any step. And then she got anxious as well and just sat herself on the ground, crying.

On the empty street where there wasn't anything that was moving, the woman looked really small and lonely sitting there by herself. She was like a crying girl who, while playing house, had broken potsherd dishes. I ran toward her by shaking off the driver who was trying to stop me by holding on to my sleeve. Within a moment I was running at a reckless speed and lifting her up at the same time and made it into the building at the opposite side of the street. The bombardment began right behind my back. We barely saved our lives.

There was something amiss about the woman. She spoke the Ham-kyung dialect and muttered something about coming from near Mount Yon-hwa but she couldn't explain exactly where she was from. When asked what her name was, she said, Hwa. Since she was from Mount Yon-hwa, I asked if the character stood for flower. She didn't know what I meant. A middle-aged man near us asked again, without even a laugh. "Is it Hwa for anger, you know, when you get angry?" When the woman still didn't answer, he said it must be Hwa for bringing on the wrath. Ugh. Don't even come near me. What bad luck… Even though he was talking that way, he got closer to her as if to touch her.

Hwa was nineteen years old. If there had not been that guy next to her, I might have gone on my way. However, I couldn't just leave her, who obviously didn't know what to do, being separated from her parents and siblings as refugees of the war, with the man next to her. She was from the remote, isolated backcountry and had never been out of her home area. I knew then that the war was much worse for people like her. The times were obviously bad, but she didn't even know how to get along with other people and live in this new world. It looked that she would eat if someone offered her food and starve if no one gave her anything.

In time of war, I felt it was doing a good deed to be responsible for Hwa's life as well as my family. I thought it was the right thing to do. At that period of time, I came to believe that notion. I thought everything would turn out all right. Was it self-conceit? I had confidence as well. But…

Grandfather suspended all his relationships in Korea and came over to America. The fact that he couldn't be financially stable, as he had anticipated, perplexed him and led him to despair. He had expected to earn his tuition and living by either doing the dishes, cleaning the hotel rooms, or pumping gas at a gas station. But in reality, it was very difficult to find a job. Being a cook was considered the top of the line. It was impossible to support his family in Korea when it was really hard for him to work and study at the same time.

At least his wife had support and aid from his and her parents. She also had relentless will to live better with her two children. So, there was less to worry about her. Hwa, who didn't have any close relatives, lacked competence and boldness and she had no idea what to do. She was raising a son, who was about aunt's age, named Won. Grandfather kept writing letters asking her to be patient in waiting for a little while.

Finally, he had managed to finish his three years of study and it was around vacation time when the news of Hwa's illness reached him. Since Hwa didn't know how to write, she had asked someone to write the letter for her. It was difficult to figure out from that poorly written letter how sick she was. In the beginning, he expected her to get better soon since she was still so young. He sent her money he had earned during the school break and told her to seek a doctor's treatment. He was concerned whether Hwa would be able to express herself well at the hospital, but what else could he do? Much time had passed while he was deeply worrying about her.

After several months, Hwa stopped sending letters. The last letter said that she had seen a doctor who gave her a prescription, but she didn't get much better. Grandfather was anxious once again. How serious was her illness? Since he had to send at least for the medicine, work became more important to him than education. He couldn't just go back. Even if he worked as a janitor in a hotel, a day's pay equaled a month's pay in Korea. Grandfather focused solely on work. Please write what illness you have. I will try to find some medicine from here. The medicine here will be better, he wrote many times over. There were no responses. Since the letters were never returned to the sender, she might not have moved; she must have been very sick.

Grandfather quit his education. He thought he would bring over his wife and children and do everything he could to bring over Hwa and find cure for her illness. If he did that, his wife would understand. No, he would persuade her to understand. He had to think of Won's future as well.

As a plantation laborer, he first brought over grandmother, father and aunt. Even that wasn't an easy process. He was helped by a second-generation Korean, who, born on the Hawaii sugarcane plantation, was keen on bringing over Koreans to America, without wanting for reason. Grandfather was able to quit the second-generation Korean's vineyard work and buy a small farm of his own. He began the process of bringing over Hwa by all means. It was a difficult task in every aspect. He had to face grandmother, who fasted to show her opposition to the idea. And further, Hwa was not legally registered as his family member.

It wasn't a question of authenticating Hwa and Won as his common law wife and son. There was no way to even verify that Hwa and Won existed in this world. Hwa came down to the south of Korea during the war without any formal identification. With the country divided into two after the war, she couldn't obtain any certificate of her existence from the north. Won's situation was no different. On what vein of the river should Won's name be attached?

Fortunately, there was the talk of how the court system would again certify those refugees of the war. Once he found out about this, he decided to ask his mother for help in taking care of the matter. Mother, I have a woman named Hwa. She is raising a son of mine named Won but I think she is quite ill. Please help me bring them over to America. It was calling for her charity, but when his mother heard about the existence of a grandson, she sought her out.

After just one visit, mother wrote to her son. Forget her. Try to erase any memory of her. I would never visit there again. She has syphilis. Mother and son refuse to be separated. Just so you know. It's better that way. Who knows whether Won is your son or not for sure? So that's it. That's how it was... She was already out of my hands. If that is so... He had decided to forget Hwa within the comfort and safety of the family, his wife, son and daughter. His mother and wife both carried a silver dagger during the war. Whatever the situation, there are women who could and who couldn't do that. Between those two types of women lay the silver dagger's sharp blade. He wanted to go within that enclosure, which women keep strictly, and push Hwa out of his mind. Further, since she no longer sent any letters, if he stopped writing to her, the relationship would gradually fade.

Three more years passed. During that time, grandfather busied himself only at his farm. It was grandmother who had to deliver the vegetables and take care of all other kinds of outside activities. Grandmother had to work with her son, rather than her husband. Other than the farm work, grandfather sidestepped around life's other happenings. He had no interest in his children's affairs. Even in the middle of the night, while smoking a cigarette in the dark yard, without hesitation he would become absorbed in one thought. The woman who ate when provided and who starved when not. The woman who stayed if told to and who came along when told to without any questions. Hwa for bringing on the wrath. Ugh. Don't even come near me. What bad luck... Even though he was talking that way, he got closer to her as if to touch her. Was I that middle-aged man?

While life was passing endlessly, a letter arrived for grandfather. He thought at first it was a prank letter because the sender was simply Won. Won? Without a last name or address of the sender. Who had a great victory? The letter was simple. Mother died. She was cremated today. I waited for three years every single day. She waited until the last moment and died. It wasn't illness; she died because she was tired of waiting. Starting today, I do not have a father. And, as if he was worried that the receiver might have forgotten Korean, he wrote in English. I hate you!

That's how he lost his son. For a while grandfather traveled in and out of Korea uselessly to seek out Won. Won never returned to his home after leaving it with his mother's ashes. Like Won who had disappeared, grandfather wanted to let himself go. He lived by earth as if he were a nonexistence. The earth was he and he was the earth. The earth which would moan and wiggle by the strong wet wind. The earth that would reveal a bit of new earth when drought causes a crack.

Wherever his body was, grandfather was like a tree, which resembled earth, standing in the middle of his farm. The tree only grew tall without sprouting any leaves. Trying to change grandfather who was like that, grandmother would mention something about moving. On days like that there was an earthquake and the volcano erupted. Grandfather's letter ended there and the next page was a letter written by Jae-Seung, dated two years ago.

To grandfather. I do not have much hope of having this letter delivered to you. The bundle of letters, sent to father by you which he carried around with him all the time, is so worn and faded that you can't even read some of them. Through all those years, it's hard to imagine that you have not moved even once. Nonetheless, since I have contemplated at least once to write to you, I am carrying it out. By writing this letter, I am hoping that father will give up on you. Father has now become a disabled person. He lives by drinking. When he does drink, he cries hard and talks about you, grandfather. Jae-Seung, don't lose your pep just because you don't have power and money. You have a grandfather in America, don't you? Not just any grandfather but a grandfather with a Ph.D. degree. I don't know what sort of doctor he is. I wrote a letter to that grandfather long time ago. After your grandmother passed away, I use a dictionary to write this. I hate you. Do you know what that means? Do you or don't you? I am not writing this letter to you today in hopes of obtaining power and money, which do not seem to be in my destiny. Most probably, this letter will not reach you in any event. I wanted to let you know that as the years pass what I want to say to you is resembling what father has said to you.

Whenever I have to struggle in life, whenever I have to put my insignificant life on the line for a shabby success and a small hope, strangely there is a despair waiting for me with its treacherous mouth wide open. (I am not referring to the physical violence of poverty and obscurity.) That unresolved despair at any moment will swallow me and make me just like my father. Sometimes, I yearn for it. Sometimes, I want to know the origin of that despair. I do not know my mother. Father, who has lived like a vagrant since he was young, doesn't have much memory of my mother. It must have been a meaningless relationship.

Sometimes, I think that it is fortunate since I do not have the ability to be responsible for them. Sometimes, that lack of knowledge becomes my darkness. That goes for grandfather as well. Strictly speaking, it seems so unfair to carry darkness to stand for things that I do not have responsibility over. Father was trapped in I hate you and lived his life as your subordinate. I intend to use the same statement and achieve separation from my bloodline.

In reverse, I intend to accomplish cutting the cord that connects my embarrassing father, who you see as a subordinate, to you and the cord that connects me, your son's son, to you. After today, I will never write to you again. I do not know why my father gave me your name. I want to be free from the name, which hang around my life like an amulet. Right now, I would like to have a name that is the most precious in this world, if that is possible for someone like me...

While I was reading the letter, father, who had finished his reading, was looking out the window. The window was wall-papered with the darkness and he was looking at his reflection, which was looking at him. Having finished reading, I folded all the pieces and put them back into the envelope. I pushed the envelope to the middle of the table and turned toward the window. As if it had been waiting, my reflection looked back at me. I looked back at its dark face. There was sound of steps coming from the staircase, but we didn't dare to look back.

Jae-Seung came closer and stood between father and me. I couldn't sleep, he said and ran his hand through his hair. That was like grandfather's long held habit. My reflection didn't have to look around to know it. Jae-Seung followed our gaze and looked out the window. Three pairs of eyes wandered, struggling not to entangle within that small pane of glass. After roaming around for a bit, as my wandering became nauseous, I realized the limit of perseverance. I went out of the boundary of my reflection and took a look at that of my father. It was a lot older than I had thought. I thought of Suu Kyi's photographs. In her photographs, one could see the growth ring of life beyond the skin. My father's reflection looked at me. Momentarily, we sought out the gaze of the reflection in the middle. All three glances came together. Inside the dark window, three reflections were looking at each other. Sometime later, my father shattered that. He turned and looked up at Jae-Seung.

"Jae-Seung, grandfather wanted to sell this farm and give it to you. Although it is no longer a farm... However, I wondered, rather than sell it, if we could build a small hospital. For treating Koreans, like your father... You will need your own freedom as well since you must be seriously thinking about enrolling in a medical school. As for your father, changing the environment and being treated near his family, his condition might improve... I know it seems all rather sudden, it is really a concept I have been planning for a while. Unless you do not have any interest in the field, which I don't think is the case..."

It was very like father. I got up and went to the kitchen. In order to make some tea for Jae-Seung, I set the kettle on the stove. In life, something that might be disgustingly unappealing to someone could be really wanted by someone else. Life gets entangled on its every flow to the faraway dark river. Perhaps a hundred million years from now, all the tributaries might become one body of water. Perhaps that's what fairness is all about.

While waiting for the water to boil, I called Suu Kyi. It seemed that she had been waiting for my call. Right away she asked whether talks were going all right. Okay, I answered. Now it was my turn to have a talk with my father.

I carried the tea to the table. I could hear loud splashing from the bathroom where Jae-Seung was washing his face. There had been times when I needed to wash my face loudly. I was sure father, too, had instances like that once in a while in his life. And Suu Kyi would have quickly lifted her camera for the moments like those. I placed Jae-Seung's tea where I was seating and took a seat next to it and asked my father.

"If grandfather had the opportunity, what sort of name do you think he would have given to Jae-Seung?" Father spoke, "He would have still named him Jae-Seung." I thought about what uncle had said. Father must have loved him considerably... "But grandfather didn't have just one grandson..." Father said, "Don't blame your grandfather too much. It's all workings of life as the flow of a long river through the darkness and time. And as for you, there's nothing to worry about since you will be going out to the wide world and fulfilling your wishes..." "What does *jae seung* mean any way?" I asked.

"*Jae* means again and *seung* has many meanings. To connect, to climb, to win... It could mean living wherever, either in Korea or America or wherever your new world might be, reconnecting through bend by bend, climbing and climbing, and winning the drown of the time."

TRANSLATED BY EUNHWA CHOE

Young K. Hahn, a member of the P.E.N. Club, is a winner of the New Writer Award from the Korean Literature Association of New York (1994), the Overseas Korean Foundation Literature Award (1999), and the New Literature: Poetry Award from the *Korea Times of New York* (2000).

Elsie Hyeryung Kim

The Swallow

THOUGH IT WAS March on the calendar, the evening wind digging into his nape was still as sharp as a razor blade. It must be already spring in the hometown. Daydreams can help, sometimes. He talked to himself and tried to whistle the melody of "Swallow" pursing his frozen lips. But it sounded like a broken whistle. This time he tried a Korean song, "My home is the southern sea," but his neck was shrinking like that of a tortoise.

Like any other night, he slowed down far away from the INS building and looked around. It certainly was his intention to go early and claim a space in the line, but he also needed to avoid being noticed as a habitual visitor by the guards or others.

Fortunately, he could count twenty or so of people already sitting curled up side by side against the wall. Wearing layers over layers of clothing, they all looked plump like a bunch of snowmen. Woolen sweaters and gloves, hats, and overcoats... And even some sleeping bags.

He went to the end of the line, spread a piece of old newspaper and sat on it. He covered himself with a blanket, settled down and looked around himself. Some were eating, some were reading, and some women were completely absorbed in knitting with their fingers poking through finger-cut-gloves. Everybody was so well prepared to spend a night there.

It hadn't been long since he started this business. At least in his thought the last three months were only "for a while." Just for a while. It's better than nothing. Just temporarily. Until I find a job. When he first came to INS, he never dreamed it could turn out to be a moneymaking job. It just happened that he wasted his trip two days in a row to renew his work permit, and then on the third day when he lost his real job, it became his job that didn't require any work permit. The generous America! Oh, whatever. As long as he could send some money to his family. As long as it could buy some food for his wife and children.

Why the nights go so slowly when one keeps vigil. Like a saucy little birdie, the hands of the night clock seemed to hop only a few steps and rest, a few more steps and drink water, and then a few more steps to stop and look up the sky. The stars on the sky he peeked through the woolen hat and muffler were twinkling as tiny as stepping-stones for little birdies. His heavy eyes were stepping on the stars one by one, but were constantly falling down to a swamp of sleep.

On the arms, legs and shoulders of his wife, so many little birds were sitting with all their red beaks wide open. Although she was happy to tell him that the swallows came back, a good half of her face was shadowy. He woke up as he held out his hands to touch the shadow on her face.

Ten forty five. The line that started at the entrance was now making a turn at the corner of the building. In spite of so many people gathered, the night was as quiet as a mouse. Indeed, these people must have left their mind somewhere else, keeping only their skins standing in the line. Otherwise, how can anyone do this in his or her right mind? Only hazy white breaths from the people were moving shapelessly in the cold darkness. He tried to twist his body that felt stiff like a log. Even if his mind was traveling somewhere else, he wanted to make sure he still had a sound body when his mind needed to come back. But it was still too early for his mind to come back.

He saw his wife again in far distance. He walked toward her with a flower bouquet in his chest, but somehow he was not getting any closer to her. Instead, he was only getting tired and breathless. When he woke up sneezing and all sweaty, it was twelve fifty. The line had completely wrapped the building once and its tail was now resting on the street. Five more hours to go. It made him feel better that at least the date was now changed.

Sleep again. He heard some birds. They were holding hands together: he his wife's and she their child's. They were running somewhere following the birdsong. He didn't know what they were going to do after catching the bird, but they were running this way and that way until he woke up with ear-tearing screech of a horn. It was only the people's laughter, but the yellow traffic sign he saw at the end of the dream remained burnt on his retina. The silhouette of a family: a man, a woman, and a child holding hands together and running like crazy. It was the sign one could easily find on the freeways near Mexican border where many illegal immigrants are expected. Just like "Caution Deer" signs on the mountain roads.

The eastern corner of the sky was brightening. What were they going to do with the bird? Did he think the bird was a swallow? And a swallow can bring a gourd seed? The lucky, magical gourd seed? He stood up, shaking head to erase the silly thoughts along with the blood-freezing image of immigrants. Now was the time to start the day's work. Sore senses ran through his numbed legs like electricity, and then sharp pecking pains started to move up from his soles.

Five ten. The line had already wrapped the building three times. Foolish people. Waiting there so long frozen stiff like fish in the supermarket. They'll never get their turns. They say they take at most two hundred people every morning to process their paper.

As he looked around, clicking his tongue with pity, a young man came in sight of him and he held his breath. A young man with a crutch was just passing in front of him. By instinct, he knew the young man was a Korean. From the dandy outfit and the cast filled with scribbles, he could easily imagine the young man in a ski trip with his young and merry friends. What a nice life! And to prove his instinct, he saw some Korean letters on his cast, which read "lucky leg." Lucky leg? Huh! Let's see how lucky it is.

The young man was standing at the closed entrance and was looking dumbfounded at the unbelievable length of the line.

Comes only an hour before the opening, and still wants to take care of his business, huh! He waited for the young man to see him. Just speak to me. Or, just see my eyes at least. But the young man who was walking in his direction suddenly turned and began to walk back to the front. Do I have a competitor in the front? He had his day's income walking away before his eyes and yet he couldn't cry out for it. He was frustrated at his stupid situation. Soon he heard some voices from the front. I came at six thirty. I at seven p.m. It seemed the young man was asking the people how early they came. You mean, seven p.m. last night?

It was easy to imagine the young man's face: his round surprised eyes and the mouth wide open like a cod. That's how he came and wasted his trips in the beginning, too. From such a fool, maybe I can get at least one hundred dollars. No, he might pay even two hundred dollars without any bargain. He silently moved his lips to pronounce "one hundred dollars" and "two hundred dollars." He managed to stay in this business for almost three months, but the first word was still difficult to push out. His throat always parched up and he stammered miserably. And of course, he did not want to say it in Korean in this case. That wouldn't help his speech. Plus, he had no intention to sell his national pride.

It was already close to the opening time. He noticed some guards in uniform walking out to organize the line. But then the young man... With his shoulder drooped low, the stupid fellow was walking out to the parking lot! Such a one-track mind! Have you ever heard something called "short cut"? The thought that the whole night's work would go down to drain made him boil over the young man. He was mad at the young man as if it were all because of him that he couldn't catch the swallow in his dream, let alone waiting in cold for the whole night. "Hello, hello, hey you! You stupid birdbrain!" He called, shouted, yelled, and screamed with all his might, in silence, after the receding young man.

Instead of the young man, however, a homeless person who seemed barely alive got up from his sleep under a bridge and came in his direction. He recognized the homeless person with his disheveled hair and the cart full of junk. Since the early spring, the homeless person always appeared around this time when the line had grown long enough so that he could easily collect money just following the line. The homeless person blocked the young man as if he had chosen him for the first business of the day, and then began to walk toward him with the young man in front of himself.

His heart began to pound. This time, this time, I'll open my mouth. I will. Definitely. No, I'll make him trip on my leg, if I have to.

Cuanto? Suddenly, he heard a whisper in his ear. Huh, a bold front! And what a prejudiced snob, not recognizing his fellow Korean! But he heaved a sigh of relief, and for the first time in his life, thanked his dark skin and big round eyes. It would have been too humiliating to be recognized and asked in Korean.

"Two hundred," he was about to say, but he had to gulp down the words. A guard passed just in front of his nose. "One hundred." He couldn't help but getting angry with himself for lowering the price without a word of negotiation. So he made a resolute face and looked away. Over the rooftop of the building before him was a white half moon making its faint appearance. "Fifty." This time the young man spitted out in a rather low and firm voice, "Deal."

Although he felt it was unfair, he had to hurry and finish the bargain because he saw the fluorescent lights come on inside the glass doors. But then, what a dimwit! The young man's hand groped in the inner pocket of his leather jacket and took out a checkbook. Why not an American Express! "Cash!" he said in an angry and rather loud voice wincing a little.

"Well, I don't have any cash...." The young man murmured with a perplexed face. "Cash!" He snapped out fiercely as if taking out all his anger and grudge at once. "Then, then, could you just wait for me for a while?" The young man stammered and nearly begged. "Oh, hurry up!" He made a blunt answer, swallowing a bitter sigh.

The line stirred up and began to move. Soon the door will open, and his turn will come... And then, it will all go down to drain.... The night's wait, the bargain... everything.

It seemed the young man was just about to begin his search for an automatic teller machine. As he watched the young man run and limp, whirling his crutch in the air, he had to hold himself tight not to volunteer to run for him.

One minute, two minutes, the opening time was getting close. And so was the homeless person who started collecting money in the front of the line. But then, the young man whose face barely showed up, for some unknown reason, suddenly turned around and began to run in the other way. That jerk!

Finally the doors opened, but the young man didn't come back to him until only five or six people left before him. "Here we go!" The young man spoke panting and held out the money. He didn't hear the young man's murmur until after he rushed to put the money in his pocket without counting. "What a shame! It's so difficult to make changes around here."

Come to think of it, the young man must have run limping only to break a twenty-dollar bill from an ATM into two ten-dollar bills. Oh, what an atrocious character! He was clenching his teeth to keep himself from jumping over the young man and breaking his yet-unimpaired leg when the homeless held out his dirty hand at his nose. The homeless said rather generously.

"Tomorrow's okay, you know, if you don't have changes."

In a moment of bewilderment he dropped a ten-dollar bill from the young man on the hand of the homeless. As he left the place in a hurry, a thought occurred to him. Should I make a suggestion to him? Instead of begging, he should make money by waiting in the line with me. But he quickly erased the thought. Everyone has his own way of life, and that should be respected.

Kicking some old newspapers rolling on the windy street, he walked into the city's forest of buildings. On one of those newspapers was the news about a swallow festival: to welcome the swallows coming far from the south... without any proper paper works and immigration procedures.

Until it turned winter again and the birds began to hurry back to the south, he didn't know "swallow" was also the nickname for the homeless.

Elsie Hyeryung Kim, a resident of Southern California, has had her poems published in two works, *Trivial Scream* and *The Stars Are Dangerous*. She has won short-story contests from *Hyundae Munhak* (1994) and the *Los Angeles Times* (1993).

Seulhee Ahn

A Tale from the Cornfield

1

THE FOX USED to come by the backyard every night. Beyond the briar-bush boundaries which surrounded our yard, and the cornfield farther out, he made his home in the forest somewhere. He lived with his mate, who had captured the evening's orange glow in her fur, and their adorable kits.

Each night, like an unrestrained wind blowing over the plains, he crossed the cornfield and stole into our backyard. He greedily ate the leftover dog food I deliberately scattered around my kennel at the base of the acacia tree. He would save a large chunk of it. After he was done eating, he would grab it in his jaws and hurriedly retrace his steps to the cornfield. Probably he was saving it for his kits. When everyone else was asleep during the night, in the darkness, I would hide myself behind the family-room sliding doors and waited patiently for his appearance.

If you've ever awakened in the middle of the night and looked out the window into the opaque darkness, you will know this sensation. When the dematerialized stillness of the dark is steadily observed, an uneasy feeling, like a fish bone lodged in your throat, inflames yet numbs your being...

However, any such feelings of mine would disappear completely when that fellow made his appearance. My ultimate pleasure came when I observed the fox moving about the yard unaware of my presence. He looked very alert and at the same time naive in his acts. To maintain my sense of benevolent superiority, I deliberately sacrificed a share of my dog food to him each day. Strangely enough, sharing my food with him like this created a sort of bond between us. Akin to a secret love, I developed a keen sense of affection for this fellow. The feeling sprouted like a corn kernel sown by a farmer in the early spring. In times thereafter, the distant sound of his footsteps would come as a prelude to a joy in my heart like a lamp brightening—a lamp light... He probably never experienced this warm light that seemed to push away the deep, thick, swamp-like darkness. Nonetheless, I became comfortably used to the lamp light which accompanied his approach. Could this have been called a relationship of sorts? Perhaps. Any acquaintance is an intersection of fates like the point where the tip of a branch meets the air.

One time, he and I came upon each other coincidentally during the day. Well actually, we glanced at each other from a distance. It was when a lark flew across the clear azure sky. I was out on a walk with the old man Park in the cornfield. The corn stalks were growing with a deep-green tint and were competing in height. I was following the old man Park around the perimeter of the many acres of the cornfield. He was deep in thought and I followed hurriedly. I stopped abruptly as the sweet fragrance of honey-suckle reached my nose. In the distance, near the edge of the cornfield where the forest meets it, the fox and his clan were frolicking before my eyes. I could not hide my excitement. I barked as loudly as I could and ran toward them. Startled and yet calm, he watched my approach for a minute. With sudden haste he escorted his mate and kits, and they disappeared into the forest. I continued toward the forest, but they were long gone. The fallen leaves crackled under foot as the fresh smell of the greens and the moist silence engulfed me.

2

Last night, the fox did not come to the backyard. I wondered what had happened. I spent the whole day thinking about him. Even that day we had seen each other in the cornfield, he had come to the backyard that night. He had come later than usual, well into the deep night. I had observed him as he glanced around, full of confidence and courage. He almost never missed visiting my abode even in the rain or snow. Although there was the possibility he had come by after I'd dozed off, tired of waiting for him.

"Keng-keng-keng!!!"

Suddenly, I recalled a noise I'd heard last night in my sleep. It seemed to have come from the cornfield. It had given me an awful premonition, and yet I'd been unable to escape from my slumber. I got mighty curious and had a great urge to go out to the cornfield and investigate. However, I could not break the rules. I was restricted from going out beyond the fenced area without supervision. My previous owner had brainwashed me. My desire for freedom had been replaced by the duty to watch for tres-passers. Even after he had moved away and left me behind, my force of habit remained. Perhaps it was my only choice, not an unseen chain, as it would have been for anyone long-indentured as an obedient and loyal servant.

"Bok-Dong!"

Finally, the old man Park came out to the backyard after staying cooped up alone in the house most of the day. He called out to me. I'd been killing time chasing squirrels, and when I'd tired of that, searching for traces of the fox, just in case he had stopped by last night. I ran toward the old man flipping my tail with delight.

"A dog's life is the ultimate life, is it not?" he asked. "Taking naps at your pleasure. Having so much fun chasing squirrels, you do not even realize the day has gone by, do you? I bet you don't feel trapped in the backyard at all."

After his son and daughter-in-law woke up their sleeping children at dawn and left for their carryout store, the lingering old man was expected to look after the house. Through the window, he gazed out at the backyard now and then. It seemed to be the only activity he did while at home. The old man Park graciously smiled at me. He petted me gently with his hand, his thick coarse fingers combing my fur. When he smiled, his dark spotted old face wrinkled even deeper.

"Shall we go for a walk near the cornfields? Bok-Dong, come, follow me and don't stray."

The old man started our daily ritual walk with same old phrases. He let out a dry cough as a signal to begin our walk, guiding me. I would wait all day for him to appear for the walk. Even then I got very impatient at times and complained loudly for the old man to hear as I followed him closely.

"Old man, to be honest, it is difficult to respond to the name Bok-Dong. My real name is Elvis. It's Elvis," I said.

The old man Park ignored my complaints and walked on at a brisk pace. I felt bad, however. It was unfair that I could understand human language far better than he could understand mine. I could only lament our Creator's division of species and its limitations. But I mainly blamed the Nelsons for making me put up with a name like Bok-Dong. The Nelsons had been my original owners.

In the beginning, everyday seemed like a honeymoon for the couple. They had two sons, one right after the other. They still seemed to get along very well. All of a sudden, they found they were no longer compatible. The next thing I heard, each had a lover! After frequent fights and arguments, they finally decided to divorce. When the Parks came along looking to buy a house in the neighborhood, the Nelsons were only too happy to sell theirs and go their separate ways. None of them wanted a dog in their new apartment. So they tagged me to this house with its two-acre lot, and handed me over to the Parks without even remembering to tell them my name.

I had only a vague image of parents and other siblings and had been attached to the Nelsons since I was a puppy. After the Nelsons departed separately, I felt ruefully depressed. I lost my appetite for food and stayed cooped up in the dog house. I was bitter that the humans could simply have abandoned me like that—talk about traitors! As time passed, my feelings of love and hate hung low in the air like a damp rain cloud. The snare of my

SURFACING SADNESS

gloom oppressed me. It meant a severance between me and the rest of the world. I was so overwhelmed with sadness that I became totally incapacitated. I had neither desire nor energy to do anything. Eating, drinking, and discharging all seemed superfluous. When I could no longer whimper with longing for the Nelsons, I simply laid my head on my forepaws and listened to the lonesome sound of the breeze for many days.

During that time, the old man Park would come by and place a piece of steak near my dried-up nose, patting me gently. Although I'd been crazy about steak previously, I had no appetite for it now and kept turning my head away. Nonetheless, the old man would visit me several times a day. He would sit before the doghouse and offer various foods and fresh water. His daughter-in-law, Mrs. Park, just noticed how I wouldn't eat.

"Perhaps he is sick," she said.

But surprisingly, the old man knew precisely how I felt.

"You are heart broken, for sure, being separated from the people you knew as your family...you poor thing. I know how you feel. Of course I know. In fact, not long ago, I had to send my old woman away...to the other world, never to return."

The old man Park, who had been looking at me and unburdening himself, looked up dimly at the far-away sky with wet eyes. The green leaves formed complimentary colors with the blue of the sky as they trembled in the breeze. I didn't really know what he meant by sending his old woman away, or by the other world? It seemed as far away as the place where the Nelsons had gone. Perhaps it was in the sky where the old man was looking? Suddenly, I felt a sense of intimacy with this stranger. Vaguely, I realized I could become close to him with sadness and loneliness as our common ground.

"Hey there, at any rate, don't you have to eat something to maintain yourself if you are going to live? Well, now, since I don't know your name, I must give you one, eh?" he said.

As if to shake off his sadness, he deliberately brightened his face and voice.

"Bok-Dong! How about Bok-Dong? 'Bok' for good fortune and 'Dong' for a child. Now, that's a fine name, I would say."

Sensing his satisfied demeanor as he slapped his thigh made me happy in return. I took his offer of the bul-go-gy steak by champing off a big piece and then licking his coarse palm. He laughed heartily.

From that day on, my life improved tremendously. That same night after the old man gave me the new name Bok-Dong and a new human friendship, the fox came to visit for the first time. It was more than a coincidence. A friend of Mr. Park had told him about his own dog's valor. Apparently, the friend had a dog inside his house when a burglar broke in. The dog attacked the burglar and repelled him successfully. After hearing that story, Mr. Park decided to keep me in the house at night also. It wasn't easy not to be able to relieve myself during the night. But it wasn't so bad either, since the fox began coming by every night due to my absence from the backyard. Once I had recovered my energy and spirit, I concluded that life was unpredictable.

3

"Hi," said Mr. Ayers.

As the old man and I were turning a corner on the narrow path where the briar bushes meet the edge of the cornfield, our next-door neighbor Mr. Ayers waved his hand. He was working in his small vegetable garden.

"Ah, hi," replied old man Park as he abruptly stopped in his tracks.

He retrieved a hand from behind his back and gestured just as Mr. Ayers had done. That was it. As always, they would look at each other and smile a little before they went their separate ways, a bit embarrassed, as in a promised union unfulfilled. Mr. Ayers would go on with his weeding and old man Park would continue his walk toward the cornfield with me.

"Gee, if only I could speak English well enough to greet properly..." the old man complained.

I gave him a toothy grin. If humans dismiss dogs as mute creatures, they are wrong. Dogs are born with abilities to understand language exceeding those of many humans. For Mr. Ayers and old man Park, their different languages made communication impossible. For dogs, it would not have been a problem at all. Dogs are amazing creatures who can understand the language of any human nationality. I wonder how many verbose humans really understand that non-verbal communications portray the true inner thoughts of the speaker better than what is said. I've heard there are humans who mistreat and abuse dogs. Dogs would not lie to or plot against others. We are very clever and can sense feelings just by looking in the eyes of others.

I was surprised at how much Mr. Ayers and old man Park resembled each other. Humans must age similarly despite racial differences. The frosty hair, the annual ridges on their foreheads depicting the happiness and sadness of life gone by, and the melancholy of the sunset in their facial expressions were all alike.

Where the narrow path ended, the old man came to a halt. The cornfield, which reminded me of the open ocean, had come into full view. The deep-green leaves stirred with a rustling noise and made waves like the ocean.

I had seen the ocean only once. A few years back, on a hot summer day, the Nelsons put me in the back seat of their car and drove to a beach about three or four hours away. When I saw the ocean the first time, I thought about the cornfield. And later, the great open space of the cornfield reminded me of the ocean. Or perhaps it was the sky which looked as if it had been transported from above the ocean?

Before long, the cornstalks would reach maturity. Then they would be taller than a grown human and would buoyantly obscure the sky.

"Let's go this way for a change," said Mr. Park.

After he surveyed the cornfield with narrowed eyes, the old man took the path to the right which was opposite our usual direction. Along the perimeter of the cornfield, the wildflowers and ripening raspberries formed an appealing mixture of colors.

"How are you?" the Talking Oak Tree said gladly as we passed beneath her branches which were trembling in the breeze above her head.

She was looking out toward the cornfield. Again, as always before, the old man did not hear her and passed by. I stopped.

"How are you? I haven't seen you for awhile," I said formally to her.

Once the old man had looked up at the tree and mentioned how some of the twists of the aged tree's trunk resembled the face of a woman. As he'd mentioned, she did look rather peculiar for a tree.

"You don't pass here anymore. I always see you and the old man walking in the distance. I envy your mobility and ... I am very lonely."

The breeze flowed through her branches at that moment. She shivered as if in self-pity.

"That really isn't my fault, you know," I responded feebly in embarrassment.

"I know, but I grow tired of living in vague expectation each day. Even the birds don't come back to my embrace any more."

She expressed her sadness and loneliness through her whole body. In the distance, the sound of a train's whistle could be heard.

"Bok-Dong! Hurry up! The train is coming," the old man called to me desperately from a distance as he looked back in our direction.

I wanted to say something more to her in sympathy. However, I had to say goodbye in a hurry. I glanced back and saw her standing forlornly, an empty nest in her bosom and her back to a beautiful sunset in the western sky.

4

Choo-Chooo!!! The sound of the train traveling on its tracks came closer and closer. It passed by a hill near where we were standing.

"One, two, three, four... twelve, thirteen, fourteen! Bok-Dong, this one has fourteen cars," observed Mr. Park. The noisy freight train passed by fast while a childish excitement lingered on the old man's face. Then its tail was hidden by the cornfield. When the fading noise of the train disappeared altogether, a sparse silence reflecting the empty sky enveloped the cornfield. Above the field, a hawk spread its wings high in the sky and traced a slow circle. Having lost its warmth, the sun was settling slowly in a golden western sky.

"Bok-Dong. A long time ago, near the elementary school I used to work at as the principal, there was a railroad going through the town. Sometimes when I was in my small office tending to my duties, I could hear the music class next door. The children would be singing while the teacher played an organ... There was a children's song I particularly liked. Listen, now."

The old man cleared his throat with a small cough and started to sing in his husky voice. He walked toward home while singing, "In an old cottage near the railroad a-co. Although the sound of the train is loud, a baby sleeps well, a baby sleeps well."

This was the first time I ever heard him sing. I got excited and, in a dancing mood, I ran ahead in jolly skips.

"Caw! Caw!" yelled a group of crows as they suddenly flew out from among the thick leaves of the cornstalks near us. The startled old man expectorated in anger and shook his fist at the flying crows.

"Be gone bad-omen carriers! Get away from here! I still have sometime left before I go to the other world. Shoo, shoo!"

At that moment, I felt an awful premonition as the smell of blood touched my nose. I expected a dead deer, rabbit, or pheasant, all of which I'd encountered in the cornfield lately.

However... oh no!... I doubted my eyes. I could see the bloody fox dead in the hollow of the cornfield.

"Isn't this a fox?" Mr. Park said. "The poor thing! It looks like someone shot him."

The man licked his tongue as he looked down at the body. I recalled then the unusual noise I'd heard last night. My heart jumped. Now I understood the unexplained deaths we had encountered before in the cornfield as well as the strange cry I'd heard last night in my slumber. It was the wail of the fox's mate.

In the next moment, there was a rustling of leaves and a stranger—a young man with a camouflaged hat—emerged from the cornstalks. He had a long gadget of some sort which I had never seen before. My instincts told me that he must be the one who had killed the fox, my soul companion. Anger and hatred welled up inside my heart. I barked hard as I dashed toward him with all my strength. Ashen with fear, the man lifted the gadget and aimed at me.

"No, no! Don't shoot, young man. Please, put down the gun," the old man yelled desperately in Korean as he waved his arms.

Bang! As I swiftly leaped into the air and nailed my jaws into the hunter's arm, I heard an earsplitting cry.

5

The hunter, who had fallen hard on his behind, came by to see old man Park's son that night. The younger Mr. Park and his wife usually came home after dark with the smell of hamburgers in their clothes. They were eating dinner with their children, eleven-month-old Joo-Hee and three-year-old Joo-Hyung. Both children had been in daycare from dawn until dusk. Old man Park was, of course, also present.

After ringing the bell, the hunter began to complain loudly about the old man and me as soon as the younger Mr. Park came to the door. He explained that the time around sunset, with dusk creeping in, was the best time to hunt. That was when the deer, foxes, and rabbits emerged from the cornfield. The fact that the old man and the dog had picked that time of day to walk was especially bothersome to him. He could not hunt stealthily because of that. There had been a prior occasion when he'd momentarily mistaken the old man for a deer and nearly pulled the trigger of his shotgun.

He told Mr. Park to warn his father not to take walks near the cornfield. It could be very dangerous. As he spoke, he eyed me with fear as I barked loudly behind Mr. Park while barring my teeth ferociously. The hunter showed his torn sleeve and told an exaggerated version of what had happened earlier that evening in the cornfield. He added, pointing his finger at me, that a vicious biting dog shouldn't be roaming around loose. I should be leashed, or confined.

"I am sorry," was all Mr. Park said to the hunter after listening to his complaints.

Mr. Park came back to the dinner table after the hunter had left.

"What was the hunter carping about?" the old man asked cautiously when he saw that his son's face was red with anger.

"Can't you guess what was he saying?" his son replied. "He complained that the way you take walks with the dog is interfering with his hunting. The bastard was yelling at me, and I didn't do anything. Dad, if you have nothing to do, just stay inside. Why do you have to roam around for no reason? Why do I have to take crap from my neighbors? You could easily be mistaken for a deer and get shot. It's bad enough I have to work so hard in a foreign land. Why do I have to waste my little bit of free time on stupid things like this?"

Mr. Park spat out his words to the old man with great anger. The old man turned pale.

"Il-Nam, how can you talk to your father like that? With that attitude!"

Afterward, the old man stared at his son numbly. He slowly lowered his spoon onto the table. Silently, he got up and went to his room as if suctioned into it. The door closed with a loud bang. Joo-Hee burst into tears. Mrs. Park gave her a bottle for comfort.

"Honey, I am glad you lectured your dad firmly," she whispered to her husband. "Recently, he seems rather senile. Ever since your mother passed away, your dad has not been himself. He looks utterly depressed and will not even talk to me. But he will talk to Bok-Dong as if to a human. I hear him tell him about various things which you shouldn't tell your dog."

She clicked her tongue before continuing.

"What would happen if he broke his leg while roaming around when we are gone during the day? Or what if he has a stroke and becomes bedridden? Who would take care of him? He would need to be cleaned up if he became incontinent. Well, I shouldn't say this... but since I've started... I think it would have been better if he had passed away before your mom."

"What? You mustn't say such a thing. Shush," he replied.

After lecturing his father in harsh words, Mr. Park was sitting at the table not eating much. A look of disgust spread over his face as if he had a bitter taste in his mouth. He put his index finger to his lips while looking sternly at his wife.

"Oh, it's all right," she said. "He's in his room. He can't hear us. Any way, think about it. Even if we are good to him, we cannot be like his wife. Besides, just look at my situation. He expects to eat Korean food three times a day. It's bad enough that I have to get up early to get the children's food and things ready for the babysitter. Then I have to make soups, rice and different dishes enough for all day. I even have to set the table for him. Do you know how laborious that is? When your mother was still alive, she took care of the children really well. She would do the laundry, clean the house, and even cook the dinner, in consideration of my hard day at the store. Ugh! These days don't seem worth living..."

Mrs. Park took this as an opportunity to vent her frustration. Mr. Park, who had been listening quietly, looked more tired than ever from the weight of the situation on his mind.

"Well, what do you expect me to do? I am the only son. I can't ask any of my three sisters in Korea to take him on. Besides, you know dad gave us all the money he had brought over from Korea as the down payment for this house. We owe him a lot. We do need to take care of him until he dies," he reminded her while trying to console her.

"Oh, I don't know," she said. "A life can hang on pretty long. These days living too long can be a burden, you know."

With a harsh look in her eyes, she turned her back toward her husband. Joo-Hee, who was in her arms, gave another loud cry. At that moment, I first noticed a ghostlike shadow lingering in the hallway. It vanished into the bathroom silently.

6

The sun was setting again. When a cool wind blew in from the cornfield, the white petals of the acacia tree fell like snow to the ground. They were fragile, dry petals which would crumble with the slightest touch. All day, I had been tied with a chain. Due to the events of the previous evening, Mr. Park had shackled me with an order not to leave this circle as he left for work that morning. However, my heart was filled with sorrow for the fox and worry for the old man. I was not much concerned with the deprivation of my freedom.

The old man must have felt miserable. He did not show himself all day. I wondered if he was sick? I had seen loss and an emptiness larger than the cornfield in the old man's wet eyes as he emerged from the bathroom last night. I could not imagine why the hunter liked to kill innocent animals if he had no wish to eat them? Furthermore, why was his hunting more important than the walk the old man and I took each day? It gave us immense pleasure.

Quietly, the sliding door of the family room opened. Old man Park came out to the backyard unsteadily, but with a happy grin. He came directly to me. I went up to him, my chain making a clattering noise. I licked his palm as if it had a bleeding wound.

"Bok-Dong, a kind one. Poor dog..."

He kept patting my head. His breath smelled strongly of alcohol. He got up slowly and staggered toward the dusk-fallen cornfield.

I knew instinctively that I must try to hold him back. Even if I needed to bite into his trousers, I had to stop him. I barked aloud desperately in a frenzy. I pulled hard trying to break the chain which was attached to my neck collar. It was the chain of inevitable fate. It did not let me go. Soon afterward I heard the sound of a train on the tracks. Then, as if to verify my premonition, gunfire erupted in the cornfield, "bang! bang! bang!"

It was getting dark all around me. The old man still had not returned. The empty house was without light. From the outside, it looked like a ruin in its darkness and loneliness. I stood nervously with my eyes on the cornfield which was now invisible in the darkness. The full moon began to rise above the cornfield. Finally, when the moon seemed to hang from the branch of a tree illuminating the backyard, I could no longer suppress the sadness welling up in my throat.

"Woooo!... Woooo!"

Looking up at the full moon, I felt certain it had shone like this since the earth's beginning. Then I howled the uncontrollable passion in my broken heart as my ancestors, who had once lived in the wilderness as a pack, had done for millennia.

"Woooo!... Woooo!"

TRANSLATED BY EUNHWA CHOE AND RICHMOND ALLEN

SURFACING SADNESS

Seulhee Ahn is the winner of the Washington Literature Award (fiction) and the *New York Korea Times* Literature Contest (fiction). Ahn has published her short story in the *Ja Yu Moon Hak*.

SHORT STORIES

Mia Yun

The Carp
Chapter 15, from *House of the Winds* (1999)

AS CHILDREN, WE always looked forward to the future. Each today was for tomorrow. Tomorrow for the next year. That was how we coped with our shabby present. In our innocence, we never doubted that the future would bring only good, savory things.

Then one day, walking down the street, I found that I was no longer thinking of the future or even of the present. My mind raced only toward the past. But the past was suddenly retrievable only through my own dim memories. Mother was no longer in this world.

It was so out of the blue. Mother's illness. It jumped out of nowhere and gripped her tightly. She was easily tired. Her legs swelled into tree trunks. Her shoes didn't fit. Grandmother, who always imagined that her body harbored myriads of illnesses, thus giving her the motive of prayer, came and took charge of Mother's illness.

She had just experienced faith healing; she had retreated into a prayer center, one of those that proliferated in the folds of hills around the outskirts of the city. At the end of ten days' fasting—"I drank only water," Grandmother said proudly—and fervent praying, she stood in front of a minister. The very moment the minister laid his trembling hand on her, she insisted, she felt a big swirl erupt inside and churn. She graphically described what happened next: she rushed to the bathroom to relieve herself. She sat sweating and trembling as all the poison she had been carrying for years gushed out. In an endless, foul, stinking stream! And with that, every little ailment seeped out of her body.

Remember that big, solid lump that had been pressing down her low belly for years? It was gone too, melted away, like candle wax! Her stomach used to be as big as Mount Nam. But it collapsed like a sinkhole, leaving folds of loose flaps around it. She felt like a newborn. So clean. So light. We should have seen her walking out of the prayer center. With a new life! Her feet had never been so light. Like they had been padded by goose feathers!

In between the sessions of bible reading and preaching and tuneless singing, Grandmother accompanied Mother to herb doctors. No Western medicine would cure Mother's illness, she insisted. Day and night, the concoction of herbs was boiled in the glazed medicine pot. She made sure Mother drank that bitter stew to the last drop. "Drink it up and pray. There's nothing faith cannot cure!"

But Mother didn't get better. Her belly started to swell. It was maddening. It was no wonder to Grandmother that Mother didn't get better. She lacked faith. "Beg God to make you better! Move him with your hot tears of faith!" On Mother's swelled belly, Grandmother applied moxa and smoldering mugwort pads which left ugly reddish burned marks on her. So single-minded was Grandmother, and so fervent was she in her belief, to our later regret we let her be in charge. We could hardly slip in a word of our opinions. Wistful, maybe we were afraid that our doubts might just kill Mother.

Soon, desperate and searching for someone to blame, Grandmother convinced herself that her spiteful husband's ghost was again at work. She reminded us of the old story. When her husband died, his belly was the size of a big pumpkin. Remember? He must be lonely for a companion. He couldn't get her to come to him so he now wanted his favorite daughter by his side. While Grandmother prayed and cursed her husband's ghost, Mother's liver was dying, poisoned by her expensive concoction.

One afternoon, I came home from school and found a huge, live carp swimming in a large plastic jar filled with water. The carp was really beautiful. Almost unworldly. Grandmother was proud that she had paid an enormous sum for it. Later, the live carp disappeared into a pot of boiling water. I still remember the strangely unpleasant smell that seeped out of the pot and permeated the house. In the old Korean stories, I remembered, carps talked and cried just like people. They were sacred fish. And Grandmother put it in boiling water alive!

After Mother drank that carp soup, overnight her belly stretched and expanded and swelled up into a fantastically huge mound. Mother could hardly sit up or breathe. As Mother moaned, lying on her side, Grandmother sang and prayed and cursed her husband's ghost. We had to literally wrench Mother away from her grip to rush Mother to the hospital. Grandmother plummeted to the floor. She cried.

The day he was leaving for France, on the way to Kimpo Airport, Brother stopped to see Mother at the hospital. He looked so young. He had a new haircut. I don't know why, but I suddenly remembered the day he graduated from high school. How he had seemed embarrassed about the presence of Mother and me outside his classroom. When he saw us smiling and waving through the window, he quickly ducked his head. I wondered if it was Mother's old-fashioned dress that shamed him. Or the humble chrysanthemums we had brought for him instead of a fancy bouquet of red and pink carnations with a willow branch of velvety buds. Or the lack of a camera in our hands.

Just like that day when Brother graduated at the top of his class, Mother was proud of him. He was going to France on a scholarship for a year of research. I don't remember what words Brother and Mother exchanged. It was the unspoken words I remember. The fear.

Mother always loved Brother in a different way. If her love for us daughters was a jubilant and demonstrative one, her love for him, for her only son, was a stoic one. It was a constant and quiet vigil. An absolute devotion. Perhaps that is the way mothers love their sons in Korea.

Mother tried so hard that afternoon not to show tears to him. Not to weigh him down with her tears. It was wrong to show tears to someone embarking on a long journey. No matter how slim, there was always a chance that her tears might pull his plane down to the ground. Unthinkable. Then as soon as Brother left, Mother turned her face away. In her hands, she buried her feverish eyes and cried.

I don't think Brother saw that fear that erupted in Mother's eyes like black waves the moment he turned away to leave. It was the fear that she might not see him again. That she might die before he returned home. She experienced that fear again and again.

Mother was there to welcome him home one year later. We shared some good happy days. Mother cooked special dishes for him. We played cards, talked and laughed. On weekends when Brother came up to Seoul, we went out to see films. (We didn't forget how Mother used to love films.) Then he left again, this time for England. In fear and wistfulness, we went through another year. Letters and a couple of phone calls—they were expensive—kept us reassured.

A few years later, selfish in our pursuit of dreams, six months apart, Brother and I left for America to study. Mother's incurable illness was stabilized for now but we weren't sure what that would mean in the days and weeks and months to come. The fear was still there. If only digging deeper. Unspoken, but always present.

I still have the wristwatch, called Marianne, Mother bought me just before I left for America. It stopped working long ago and its strap is missing. Why a watch? Mother didn't want me to forget the passage of time. She wanted me to remember to come back home. In the taxi on the way to the airport, Mother was already crying. By the time I tore myself away from her at the airport, our eyes had puffed up like bread dough. Just as the door closed, through the fog of tears, I saw Mother standing with Brother and Sister, crying. She had always cherished her baby daughter. There in a special corner in her heart, she kept a place reserved only for her baby child. I knew that. We all knew that. Less than six months later, she took another trip to the airport to send Brother away.

It was on that child that later she relied, from whom she sought comfort and for whom her heart broke—her daughter was reaching thirty and unmarried. It was that child who took her to doctors, shopping and tended to her needs while her two other children pursued their dreams in a faraway country.

Two years later, at Kimpo Airport where I landed in the early winter morning, there was no sight of Sister or Mother waiting. I had flown all the way across the sea, dreaming of their smiling faces. The phone at home rang and rang. An hour later, Sister came running in through the revolving door. When we got into a taxi, Sister said we were going straight to the hospital. With the luggage and everything. It was a complete surprise. That Mother was in the hospital. Had been for over two weeks. Why had she chosen not to tell me until that moment? She was just like Father! All his life, Father ran away whenever he had bad news. Because he abhorred confronting us with it. He ran off, leaving us to deal with the wreckage. If he came back, it was only because he had money to buy us things, because he had titles to show us, because he had new projects brewing. For that we suffered. I wanted to but didn't ask Sister why she hadn't called and told me that Mother had gone into the hospital. I knew the answer. It was she who took care of Mother while we were away. It was she who dealt with the problems while we were away. I had no right to ask her why. I had relinquished that right when I left.

Mother lay in a near coma when I arrived at the hospital. It was a shock. A jolt. I despaired. Mother looked so small. She looked like a child. And her face was a colorless carving. I bent over her and cried. I couldn't help it. Mother must have sensed I was there. From the corner of her closed eyes, tears gushed out and tumbled down. They were from joy and relief.

That afternoon, Mother miraculously opened her eyes. When she looked at me, there was such gladness. Then with sheer will, Mother clung to life. Day and night, I sat by her side, wrapping her small hands with mine. I hoped and wished that somehow she would live. For nine days she lingered. She could barely talk. The only time she talked was to tell me that she had so much to tell me. I told her just to get better. She and I would then talk and talk. But those became her last words. The chance to talk was lost forever.

One morning, going out for breakfast, I told Mother that I would be back very soon. Mother looked at me and smiled that warm smile only she possessed. She must have known there was very little time left and must have wanted me to stay next to her. But she didn't ask me to and would never have asked me to. She wanted me to eat, to satisfy my hunger even as she was dying. When I came back, Mother was slipping into the foggy tunnel that connects life and death.

When Mother finally closed her eyes, Brother was still in America. We gave him the news by phone. I don't remember how we told him. The exact words are lost in my memory. What I remember was the deafening silence that followed. Long heart-wrenching silence. He couldn't utter a word. Not even a moan. All the light inside him simply went out. It was too much to bear. Sister and I clutched the silent receiver together and wept.

Unable to be there when Mother was buried, Brother must have suffered even more than us. Later, we would learn that Brother, alone with his grief in Texas, shut himself inside his room for days. It devastated him. As Mother's only son, he felt he had relinquished all his duties for his selfish pursuits.

Grandmother didn't come to the mountain when we went up to bury Mother on that frigid January day. It is a sin for a mother to send her child to the other world ahead of her. Maybe in that sense, Mother was lucky.

After we buried Mother, Sister and I, two motherless daughters, rarely spent time together. Each of us was an unanchored leaf boat, drifting away. Lost. We had to deal with the grief alone and apart from each other. Together, it was unbearable. And then there was the blame, resentment and regret we had to sort out and swim through. It was lonely. Lonelier than anything.

How few things Mother left behind. There were her clothes (including the immaculate Korean dresses of long ago), a sewing box, a few pieces of jewelry, a bible, some books and little notebooks where she had jotted down recipes from the radio with a pencil. Inside her black velvet coin purse, I found a roughly hewn bronze cross-wrapped with a yellow nylon cord. It connotated a shamanistic belief. Where had she got it? Who had given it to her? She must have carried it with her all the time. It was her talisman. Her fervent wish to live until we children returned.

Inside a drawer, I also found new pictures of Mother. She had them taken to send to us in America. I remembered a letter Mother had written promising to send new pictures of her. The promised pictures had never come. Now I knew why. She didn't look well in them. Her face was puffy. The puffiness buried her small features. I could hardly recognize the face in the picture. There were other snapshots. Strays. Among them was the one taken on a Mother's Day. It was the year I had entered middle school. Mother and I stood in front of cannas and gladioli. I had pinned a red carnation on her light pink jeogori. In her hanbok, neat and modest, Mother looks untouched by the passage of time. Mother leans toward me, smiling. And I stand straight, a little sullen. Why? Was the sun in my eyes? Life was now made up only of memories, not all of them clear.

A long month after Mother died, I found a lonely blue aerogramme in the mailbox. Dizzily stamped in Korean and English. It was the last letter Mother had written to me in America. It had traveled all the way to America and back. "Return to Sender," the stamp read. But the sender, Mother, was no longer here. I had not the courage to open it. I put it away in between the pages of a book. For years, the letter would remain there, unopened. As long as I kept it unopened, there seemed to exist possibility and hope. Of and for what? I didn't know.

The sense of loss and the pain from the loss never lessened with the passage of time. Weeks after, months after, they were the same. I missed her. I pined for her. I clung to the memories that I excavated, one by one, searching them out from the foggy folds where all memories go and wait to be resurrected. I clung to them even though they were only so many fragments of stone, hoping that some day, one by one, I might piece them back together as one brilliant stone.

In my memories, Mother will always remain that vibrant, young woman, perfectly happy with her children behind the blue gate of hers. She forever stands in the sunny cabbage patch. She was like one of those white cabbage flowers. Like them and like all flowers, one day it was time for her to go. That was all.

Some day, I will no longer be sad and lost. Only lonely for her.

Life is a river. It flows incessantly.

Mia Yun, currently the Korea correspondent for *Evergreen Review*, has worked as a reporter, translator, and freelance writer. *House of the Winds* is her first novel.

SHORT STORIES

Kyung Sook Park

The Caveman Who Left His Cave Country

ON VERY DEPRESSING nights, I decide to select a television program featuring extreme violence. Although it will not resolve my depression, in a strange way, by confirming the shapeless form of ugly violence, it gives me some relief. This has become an addictive habit. Those who have left their own country, like a misplaced pebble rolling along without a destination, are enveloped by the doleful sense of unease, filled with anxiety. On the day of departure, wasn't I filled with endless relief, leaving the damp and dark cave? These days, the daily newspapers are covered with the stories of boiling contents of the cave. Hopefully, the surge of the boil will reach its climax and lift off the lid of the cave, turning it into light streaming valley and not a cave. Perhaps I should have lived there forever, weather it's a dark cave or not, as a native stone. Since I do not know the difference between the cave's inside and outside environment, I wouldn't know the fact that I lived in a cave.

For the iris, which is so used to the pitch darkness, it naturally takes some time and effort to adjust to the brightness of this land. At this point, I am too tired of this onset of depression and am seeking some violent and cruel television programs using the remote control. Tonight, the History Channel has on a documentary about Holocaust. In the dusky black and white film, the Jews who were stripped of their clothing were being led into the gas chambers, looking grave and sorrow stricken. Before a very thin old man with his private parts covered by his hand, there was a young stout woman holding a hand of a child with the dark pubic area exposed. It was as if she were asking what was there to be embarrassed before an oncoming death.

SURFACING SADNESS

The next scene showed a pile of decomposed bodies. There was a close-up of fluid oozing out of noses and eyes of the bodies, which were stacked like crates. The bodies deplete of fluid looked like roasted sparrows and just as pitiful. At that moment, I had to close my eyes, my body drenched with hair-raising fear. But I couldn't turn the television off. I couldn't even figure out why I was still watching the television through slats of my fingers with gooseflesh spread all over my body. Somewhere in my body, current of pleasure, coming from beyond the fear, was emerging.

Is this the hidden cruelty in me? There was evil in me enough to find some pleasure from seeing those wretched human beings... As soon as those feelings surfaced, my eyes and nose were overflowing with fluids. Suddenly, unbearable sobs engulfed me. While I was shuddering my shoulders with tears, as when I do watching a sad drama, the television camera was focusing on the image of mustached Hitler. The narrator was saying he was the twentieth-century's ultimate evil. Before my dazed eyes, another image came on top of the mustached Hitler. This one had a beard grown as well. Quickly, my head was tangling with all sorts of thoughts. If it were the human fate to be faced with a devil every century, in what form would the twenty-first-century devil show itself? Has time arrived for us cave people, the ones called the second Jews, to suffer? Our homeland, the cave, is still restlessly rioting daily, in turn jarring the lid, which has cut off the light for a long time. Has time come for us to be persecuted? This image became clearer and clearer until he broke through the television, lashing toward me. Unconsciously, I made fists. Yes. You bastard. Now, you are my devil and there's no guarantee you will not be the persecuting devil of our cave people in the 21st century.

Shortly after coming to this vast land of America, while still dazed in awkwardness due to arriving from the cave country, the April 29th riot of Los Angeles occurred. The cave people were the target of the hatred as the rioters and looters picked through where mostly these cave people had gathered to do businesses. For me, it had already been several months since taking over a piece of white owned business, coming fresh from the cave country, like a dislodged stone relocated to this new land. There was a discord between the employee of mine and I and finally he was coming on to me as an illusion of Hitler, who couldn't tolerate Jews or other race. It was true, although it is believed to be trendy for young American men to grow mustached and beard, he seemed to look full of menace from the beginning.

He had worked for the previous owner for the last five years. It was all right when we had decided to keep him as an employee but problem arose as he looked down upon his new employer, me. Perhaps he could only look down upon this small and yellowish Asian from the cave country. When the clerk, with the blessing of good ancestral genes of fair skin, tall stature, and blue eyes, talked to me by looking down, it easily gave the illusion that he was the employer and I the employee. When he spoke his native English fast without giving much thought to the listener, it did look as if he were intentionally doing it to put me in an awkward position. It was obvious that he had no respect for me by the way he listened with his arms folded across his chest as I stuttered in inarticulate stammer. To keep my dignity as an employer, I stretched my neck from my small body as much as I could and purposely lifted my eyes to get on his nerves.

The war of the nerves between him and me escalated to the level of how I ran the business. Even though I had no prior business experience, just like Chinese people opening restaurants wherever they settle, I could only open a store with all the capital I had. Furthermore, my husband, who had lost all of his authority, expertise, and ability he had in our homeland, had less language skills than I. He pushed me forward to carry out the business while he stayed in the background. We had accidentally bought into a gourmet frozen yogurt business, which, unbeknownst to us, required some expertise. We realized this after paying off for the store to the cunning white storeowner. It was only natural that I was in a fix with our employee who could manage the ins and outs of the business with his eyes closed. As the days passed he became even more imprudent and managed the store as he wished. As I lifted my eyes further up, his blue eyes got even darker and bluer. His eyes sometimes conjured the night sea's dark fear in a terribly chilling way. I saw in the deepening eyes of his the fall of my cave country. I was beginning to subtly yearn for my native cave country, the land I had for so long longed to get away.

Even without realizing the land I was living on was a cave, I had wished to find a place of light, joy, and aridness to do away with dull, somber, and irrepressible humidity. Of course, this refers not to physical but mental humidity. With that in mind, I named my homeland a cave country. The discomforting moisture had spread wide from close neighbors to the strangers. We cannot remember why and when the unpleasant humidity began. We could only remember from disjointed memories of childhood that we used to live happily in dry air.

All the people of the cave country were politicians. Whenever they gathered, they criticized the ruling class, discussed the current events, and showed interest in how much so and so spent on his or her new chest of drawers. They were knowledgeable about which plot of land or stock should be purchased for profit. If you didn't know about these things, you were treated like an idiot. The powerful ones flared their nostrils, letting out steam and relentlessly stepped on the weaker ones' starving bellies. Whether their nostril steam rose to the sky and formed the thick clouds, which eventually became a roof-like structure covering the whole land like a lid or it began as a cave, I couldn't discern for sure. However, I was one of those who couldn't stand the moisture. The cave country people were well known for their adaptability. They adapted well to the stuffy environment, but I couldn't adapt to it. I am not perfect, but I couldn't stand something, which wasn't so. I was a freak. Everyday, my spirit would be swollen under allergic reaction and due to its itch, I would beat up and scratch and finally have fallen down.

One day, I decided to leave for a land where the light is brighter and the air is drier. I have left the cave country. There were already many cave country people who came long ago to settle down. Even as they were living here, they let out their own unique steam. Nonetheless, because the land is so immense here, no matter how much steam they generated, it never became dark or humid. I had deliberately settled in a place where blue eyed ones teemed, away from the cave country people. And now, after spending a strenuous war of nerves with a blue-eyed employee, I was looking for some mind numbing violence and cruelty filled television program to forget the strain. So today, I saw the decomposed bodies of the Jews and the fact that Hitler also had a mustache made me want to hate my employee even more.

He had to grow a mustache. I had learned that before Hitler began the genocide of Jews, a Jew had humiliated him during his college days. If a miserly Jew, blinded by his love for money, planted a grudge in young Hitler's heart, and if it caused to reveal gross evil in the future, the defiant blue-eyed one in my store, he too in his young heart, could grow grudge against our cave country people. Chill ran down my spine. He was like the young Hitler. He was a young 21-year-old college student. His blue eyes came toward me like the night sea's whirlpool. In it, my cave country people were falling.

"I heard that the former President got arrested?"

"Well, two at that."

"What's the worry? Soon they will be out as if nothing had happened. Well, I am sure they have hidden away a lot of money between the two of them."

As the young writers and poets got together on this rare occasion and exchanged some words, an elderly poet decided to join them.

"What sort of pathetic subjects arrest the father of the country?"

"What father of the country? We are in the second half of the 20th century. And besides, they are thieves."

"That's right! They are thieves. They should just go ahead and kill themselves."

As the young writers in the back get ready to refute, the elder poet raised his voice even higher.

"What nonsense! I was a government employee in Korea! I took in a lot of money as well. That's how everyone lives over there. Have you seen anyone without any faults?"

That night, those literary figures from the cave country that lived in this land were engulfed in talks about the cave country, the boiling political stories. Those who left the cave country earlier had vague, dim and hazy notion of value about their motherland. However, they were not the people of this vast land. In other words, they didn't stand on either side. They were pretty much like spectators. I myself who left the unbearable humidity of the motherland wasn't quite ready to be part of this land. One could tell by the way I tire out having confrontations with the blue-eyed one. Ultimately, I had given up a leading role in the cave country in disgust and in a laid back, irresponsible way and decided to take a harmless minor role in this expansive land. Afterward, when realizing my minor role through the employee's eyes, I couldn't bear it.

"Our immigrant literature will be over in thirty years or so. The one and a half or second generation cannot carry on literature in Korean language. When our young writers die off, no one in this land will write in Korean. That's why we have to realize for ourselves how important we are. No matter how many able writers are in our homeland, they do not know what we have felt and experienced."

With this statement, the elderly poet created a literary mood, which was marred by the talks of the presidential arrests that night.

"Immigrant literature is really terminal. When you think about it, it's quite sad. Our second generation cannot speak Korean fluently. It's really impossible to imagine them writing in Korean. Furthermore, the government here is keen on limiting immigration and with the economic boom in the homeland, there is a sharp decrease in immigration. Besides, there's a trend of immigrating back to the motherland. Then, for whom are we carrying on the literary front in this land? In addition, no one in Korea appreciates our literary circles anyway..."

I let out a sigh, unable to bear the talk any more.

"Who are we doing this for? We are just moved by our individual needs to write. Immigrant literature did not originate from nationalistic feelings or for our time. Didn't we start writing to comfort our lonely immigrant life?"

A middle-aged essayist spoke up.

"No matter how or why we started it, we have to be a source of tonic to this arid immigrant life. To those of us who are just so eager to make a lot of money, in this foreign land, we have to be responsible to our duty of idealizing them through literature. It is a writer's mission."

The elderly poet pushed up his reading glasses with his index finger and looked upon the younger members.

"But sir, in the environment where there are no professional writers, there are too many writers who see writing as a means of obtaining personal satisfaction. For example, there was a review of a poet's new volume of poetry on the culture section of a newspaper, but it is obvious that the poet didn't know who had won the literary prize featured in the column just below his interview. He had no idea whether it was a short story or a poem. It just shows how self intoxicated we are and that we have no interest in others' works."

At my somewhat offensive utterance, the elderly poet grinned.

"Are you telling your story? Yes! There is somewhat of that. Seeing everything from one's point of view is one of our culture's weak points. That's why events like arresting former presidents could occur."

The talk went back to politics of the motherland and the night's gathering ended that way.

On the television screen, Auschwitz concentration camp appeared as the narrator described the tragedy of that period. "They suffered through hard labor. The German soldiers often raped the young women. Without any warning, they were taken from their scene of labor under the auspice of taking shower and clothes were taken off and were killed in gas chambers. Their bodies were cremated in special kilns. There were educators, artists, and men of religious orders."

"There were educators, artists, and men of religious orders...hence, many who could have contributed much to the human race were wasted away..." I repeated the narrator's statement. The fact that I am here suffering in this land amused me. I, who have not contributed much to even one person, let alone the human race. Once again, his blue eyes rose up like barely contained bile coming up. For something live was violating me. To him, I was a stutter who spoke broken English and a cave country idiot who didn't know anything about running a business.

Every day, I increased the volume of my voice so as not to lose to my employee and used all my wits to pester him. I directed a lot of work for him so he could treat me courteously as an employer. It was my cunning plan not to give him any breathing space. Perhaps he has noticed that I was out to make him suffer. But what if that creates a grudge in his young heart? Just by looking at his determined poise, he has the potential to become a man of power. What if his grudge against me grows into a grudge against my cave country people, like a second Hitler? If so, I am creating a critical condition for the future of my people. I shook my head. No. I was never a nationalist. I have never given any thought to analyzing such an extravagant idea. Everything was personal to me. I have seen the current issues from my personal perspective. I am just an irresponsible person. If it wasn't that, I wasn't even curious how the country was running. It is rather pathetic, but no one whoever talked about politics in the cave country without thinking of one's personal interest.

A few decades ago, my father was responsible for a small portion of the cave country's politics. Ironically, while my father was advancing well in his political career, my school was next to the Opposition Party headquarters. We had to endure listening to the chant of "opposing the third term amendment." It was difficult to concentrate on school studies. The third term reform was the vein of my father's political up wind. I was only a child, but I knew enough about my gain to snub the chant coming from the Opposition Party speaker. My father, who had risen due to the third-term presidential reelection, bought a huge house with a pond. I was just a girl filled with dreams in that house. A while later, under an odd nomenclature of Reformation, the leader fiercely eliminated my father, who was like a loyal dog to him. The family and the wealth became scattered and I had come to grow a grudge against politics in my young heart. However, I was only a silent demonstrator who refused to vote during the elections.

The ones who have tasted the sweetness of wealth and power have a tendency to reflect that illusion all his or her life, making the current life look very shabby. In our time, power was wealth and the wealth was power. In the bitterness of being demoted from the upper crust, I had to spend my youth in loneliness. There was no pleasure when the Restoration movement died away and even when worse political era came, I didn't care. I was suffering now from my neighbors' spouting steam but didn't want to figure out why the wetness was surrounding us in darkness. Just wanting to look for brighter and drier place brought me here. And now I am just a severe individualist who is itching to scratch the body and mind over aggravating the blue-eyed employee.

"I came here in the seventies because I hated the Restoration platform of the government. My classmates have more than fifty million. Even though I am poor, living here."

The dentist talked through his mask without a break, while working on my widely opened mouth.

"Really? You couldn't have left the cave country simply for that reason. There must have been another reason. I know. It is to find someone who could criticize government without thinking about personal gain or interest. I can honestly tell you what I have learned through my own experience. During my college days, I used to know a prodigy. He was an ambitious young man who dreamed of success through passing the civil-service exam. He didn't have any inkling of political agenda held by the young men of his days. While his classmates were crying through tear gas chanting for justice, he quietly listened to music at home. While his friends were going in and out of jail, he went to the library and studied. He passed the exam. While he is still in an important position, his friends who had to go in and out of jail are starving under the shadow of the government. Well, who was more sensible? If you have truly come here because of the 'Reformation' government, then you are the one starving under the shadow and your classmates are like the prodigy I knew who successfully obtained an important post."

While I was under his lukewarm breath with closed eyes, my cavities were filed away. He took out all the stuffed tools from my mouth. I rinsed my mouth with the water from the paper cup. I absentmindedly looked at him, wanting to at least utter a few words I had patiently kept to myself. His small stature looked extremely tired under a white gown. The yellowish face covered in salt and pepper hair represented his twenty or so years of difficult immigrant life.

"Mrs. Lee! I enjoyed your short story in the newspaper the other day. Even from the beginning, I thought you had the writer's mood or shall I say nuance. I don't just look into people's mouths; I look into their hearts as well. Keep trying hard, although there isn't much literary standard here."

He opened his dull mouth wide and grinned. Through his dull grin, his breath spat out unattractively, fluttering a few white strands of hair that fell on his forehead. Due to Novocain injection, I could only grin with my numbed mouth.

"There was something of forlornness about you, Mrs. Lee. How could one who can't feel the loneliness work on creating literature? If you are looking to date, how about me? Although I am a bit old, I could at least talk about literature with you."

Embarrassed on his own, he chuckled aloud. After observing his idiotic laugh, I had to defy my numbed cheeks to say something back.

"If I were looking for someone to date, I would have found one already. You wouldn't have a chance."

Embarrassed again by my stinging rebuttal, he tried to hide it by chuckling again.

Between the steps out of the dentist office, the prodigy from my recently recovered memory trudged along. Although it was from long ago, my heart began to constrict. That prodigy, I must have liked him a lot. Was it love? You ask. Who knows! I have never used the word love. His sensibility to reality and his agility, I have liked. Because I do not have any of those qualities. Although people usually love what is similar to them, sometimes people envy what is totally opposite to them. I was obsessed with him because he was so different from me. Yes! It was merely a severe obsession. He taught me how to sneak away to home to listen to music when the streets were overflowing with demonstrating students. From time to time, he would tell me how my father's position would be useful to him when he passed his civil-service exam. But you know, when that peculiar "Restoration" movement came along, along with the wind, he disappeared without a trace. In the political change of wind, I have become a victim of it. That's how I know. I know that politics could have profound impact on individuals. But I don't know why now and then that sense of obsession would lift its head up again. Is it because you joked about dating? Frankly, I may be still dating with the worn out obsession. Perhaps now there will be no daily struggle with that obsession. For lacking the prodigy's quick thinking, I may be expressing anger toward my weak self.

While regurgitating the spoken, leftover words, the bitter chemical odor from the repaired molar was causing dry heaves. Yuck. Yuck. The dry heaves brought hollow wind through my bosom.

Perhaps since that time he may have covered over me as an outer layer. Within the outer layer, which resembles his realistic and opportunistic trait, there is a porous, useless me. Unable to balance the hard outer layer and the soft inner one, I am suffering in this vast foreign land. If the reason I couldn't stand my homeland is that I, with soft layer, couldn't live in harmony with sturdily armored people, perhaps, in this land, I cannot live harmoniously with those people who look soft outwardly but really tough inside. For all these years, it is love from youthful years that is conquering me, but it is just my obsession with that period. The obsession with the fallen things causes the despair. No, in earnest, it is the obsession with the sweet life of the upper class before the fall. Perhaps I shouldn't have let him go like that. Rather than sending him off by wearing his hard shell on me, I should have covered his hardness with my soft layer. In that way, at least one in the cave country, no, the two, he and I, could have been the ones who did not let out steam. Hence, we could have been the one who might have eliminated the humidity. If not, I could not have worn his hard layer and remain a sole being who could have been the eliminator.

I saw Tel Aviv of Israel bombarded by PLO on the television screen. The Jews, having survived through Hitler's persistent genocide, built Israel and established financial success throughout the world, but their land faces endless terrorism and slaughter. Hasn't the Biblical Exodus reached the land filled with milk and honey led by Moses?

Our cave country doesn't have to worry about terrorist from other nationals, but the daily newspaper reports other horrors. When the employee brought in the Los Angeles Times featuring hundreds who perished under the collapsed department store building in the cave country, I didn't have anything to say. He sarcastically asked whether my homeland had an earthquake. He looked down hard on me with his sparkling blue eyes. That day, I saw my small body and my cave country endlessly falling down in his undulating blue eyes. Needless to say, my mental allergic reaction reached its peak that day. I sat absentmindedly under his blue gaze, feeling my mental sneezes flowing up continuously up into the air.

No, I have disappeared before his eyes. He acted in freewill, having forgotten my existence. From the extinction of my existence under his blue eyes, the department store building's horrific collapse became clearly focused. The humidity of the cave, which was unbearable for me, wasn't actually the physical nature of it, but something that could generate fearful power. Ultimately, all the steam generated by each individual in the form of mistrust and selfishness covered the sky and seeped into the ground. The structure built on that foundation was bound to collapse. A stream of tear rolled off. My store was bright with only white customers and noisy with the words I couldn't understand. Seeing the scene through the reflection from the glass window, standing in the back, caused heartache and loneliness.

"If living was grand at home, why did we come here? Only the ones with nomadic bug would gather here. Working so hard all our lives and now we have grown into our middle age. When we finally take a breather, our children can't read Korean or even speak Korean. It's only natural they forget how to speak Korean. We were so busy making a living that we didn't spend time to talk to our children. Did you run away after being in debt? This is the land where everyone who doesn't have a reason to live in the motherland gather to live. We are becoming people who forever want to live in the cave country but can't do that any more. Rarely, when we do go back for a visit, we are faced with rudeness, starting at the airport, and the traffic jams... When we leave there again, we promise ourselves that we won't ever go back again. But when time passes, we yearn to go back again... There's no one more stupid. Ultimately, we become idiots who can't belong anywhere. Although our hearts are in the motherland, we are becoming totally immersed in the more developed culture. Can't figure out whose countryman I am..."

This woman, who was nearing her senior status and whom I just met in the supermarket, was talking to me just because I was a Korean. She even dropped the polite form of speech after gauging my younger age.

"Do we really need to distinguish which nation we belong to? We are all the same human beings on this earth. Shouldn't we just live, giving all we can wherever we are?"

She pranced upon my words, which were spoken out of embarrassment of being too quiet.

"You are talking like that because you are still young. Wait until you get older. As time passes, your yearning for your homeland gets greater. But we become idiots who can't manage to live in our homeland. If it's to be like this, we should have remained there. Having come here, we've got Westerners as daughter- and son-in-laws. Although the grandchildren have traces of our genes, by the time we see our great grandchildren, there will be no traces of us. As if we never came, there's no trace of us... If you think about it, it just feels so hollow."

Sadness filled her wrinkled face.

"Oh, that is true. Never thought of it up till then. I used to think of belonging somewhere as a burden. I was one of those who struggled to be free from belonging to a family or to a nation. I used to think that belongingness placed restraint on people, causing selfishness. Perhaps I came here to be free. To be free from all the systems and memories. But even after leaving the homeland, all those things put greater pressure on me than ever before. In other words, should I say that living with other cultures makes me more aware of my ethnicity? All the things from the past, which have contributed to the formation of myself, are being remembered more acutely. So, in the end, I have become some-one who has lost the freedom."

I let out a sigh over her graying head.

Right. Don't they say that the exiles become great patriots?

She lightly tapped my shoulder once and pushed her shopping cart toward a cashier. I would never become someone who would want to go back. And I would never regret it. I silently screamed toward her back. Her gait looked strong even in her late years. It was difficult to find a trace of immigrant life's hardship as she had complained...and I walked without strength. Totally different from my statement saying that I would never regret.

The Holocaust documentary came to an end by filling the screen with the view of the city of Jerusalem. I made a pot of coffee while looking out of the window to see the new dawn come up. I wondered if the scent of coffee was stronger at dawn when it was silent all around. I poured the strong coffee into a mug and brought it under my nose. My eyelashes became moist. Probably because of the hot steam. I took a sip. But I swallowed some other liquid along with the coffee. I was still crying. From the confused tangle of thoughts, his blue eyes suddenly popped out. The unresolved past love's pain created a deep whirlpool in my heart. And I could feel the moist air of the cave country on my skin. It was unbearable loneliness created by the fearfulness and strangeness of the new land and the yearning for the past times. I looked out at the dawn ensuing window while wiping away the tears with the back of my hand. The color of the early morning, which hasn't fully arrived, looked like me in its awkwardness of haze.

I could never be totally free anywhere. Is freedom something that is out of reach as one seeks it more? I gained a shackle of the cave country, from my departing the cave country, to seek my personal freedom. Yes. I was a part of the cave country. I was not I for my personal gain. Now, I shall cast off the hard shell of false love. If I live as my self without struggling between something that is not I and the one I want to be, perhaps I would be more tolerant in dealing with the blue-eyed one. In that way. Perhaps his blue eyes wouldn't be seen as fearful night sea, but as a sun pouring, breezy sea. After getting rid of the shell of the love and the obsession of my heart filled with unbearable exhaustion, I shall make sweat pouring love with the literature. If it is a way for me to continue to live on this land...

The hazy dawn light, which filled the window, became stronger. From the tree branch, cutting across the window, chirping of the birds tore the dawn open. With the empty mug in one hand, I was still gulping something down the throat. As a bird song tears through the dawn, the blade of the light slew into the world.

SURFACING SADNESS

TRANSLATED BY EUNHWA CHOE

Kyung Sook Park won the *Korea Times* Literary Award, Short Story Category (1994) and the Korean-American Writers Association New Author Award, Short Story Category (1995). Park debuted as a writer in Korea in 1999 with the novella *One Room*.

CONCLUSION

Korean Literature in the United States: At the Centennial

By Yearn Hong Choi

Background

ON JANUARY 13, 2003, the one-hundredth anniversary of the first Koreans landing in Honolulu is being celebrated. The migration started in early December 1902, when a group of immigrants seeking work left Inchon for Honolulu, Hawaii, to work on a sugar plantation. Their ship embarked at Shimonoseki, Japan, for a few days of inspection and health examinations. The ship then left port on the evening of December 24, and arrived in Honolulu on the night of January 12, 1903. The voyagers' first night was spent in a cabin. Thus, we celebrate January 13 as the Centennial of the arrival of the first Korean immigrants to the United States.

The first seven thousand immigrants who arrived in Hawaii between 1903 and 1905 are referred to as the first wave. After the Chosun Dynasty lost sovereignty to Japan, the immigration to Hawaii could not continue. The second wave originated a half-century later in the 1960s. The United States' immigration policy was generous to Asian people, inviting Korean students in the 1960s and 1970s to remain in the country after completing their education. Now, there are two million Koreans living in America.

The purpose of this essay is to report and review poets and writers who arrived in the second wave and who use the Korean language, not English, as their main form of literary expression. However, in between the first wave and the second wave, along with a number of short stories, three prominent Korean literary works emerged: *The Grass Roof* by Younghill Kang, *The Martyred* by Richard E. Kim, and "The Wedding Shoes" by Yong Ik Kim. These three writers were unique in that they used English as their writing medium, even though English was their second language. They were followed by Chang Rae Lee and other numerous, second-generation writers in recent years.

In the intellectual void of the 1970s and 1980s, Korean poets and writers in the United States published their works in Korean language newspapers, attended Korean churches utilizing their native language, and organized Korean literary societies in metropolitan areas such as Los Angeles, Washington, D.C., New York, Atlanta, Chicago, and San Francisco, among others. They dwelled in their own Korean language, with only a few attempting to produce literary works in English. The first publication during this period was *Jipyongsun* (*Horizon*), a small poetry magazine.

Since *Jipyongsun*

Poet Ju Whang in Los Angeles initiated this small poetry magazine with several new immigrants in the Los Angeles area who were interested in poetry writing. Joining Whang as editorial board members were Jonggi Mah and Yearn Hong Choi, who made their debut as poets in early 1960s via *Hyundai Munhak* (*Modern Literature Monthly*), the most prestigious literary magazine in South Korea. The first issue was published in 1973, with the poetry magazine drawing attention from Seoul's daily newspapers. The *Donga Ilbo* daily opined *Jipyongsun* as the first Korean literary magazine in the United States, and praised the literary efforts of Korean-Americans. Previously, overseas Korean literary magazines had been published in Manchuria and Japan in the 1930s and 1940s. However, *Jipyongsun* made history as the first literary magazine in the United States, according to Korea's daily newspapers.

Ten years later, in 1983, the Korean Literary Society of America began its annual publication of *Miju Munhak* (*Korean Literature in America*). The society was organized by novelist Sang-ok Song and poet Ho Gill Kim, both of whom immigrated to the United States. The Korean Literary Society was the first large-scale organization by Korean poets and writers in Los Angeles who claimed to represent all Stateside Korean poets and writers. Besides creating their own organization in Los Angeles, the poets began publishing their annual poetry magazine, *Oaegi* (*The Foreign Land*). Today, *Miju Munhak* is attempting to publish quarterly.

Indeed, many Korean-American poets and writers feel they need more outlets for their creative writing. In Los Angeles, the literary magazine *Woollim* (*Echo*) was short-lived, and *Munhak Saegae* (*Literary Realm*) has been published by poet Ko Won.

In the 1990s, the Korean Poets and Writers Group of the Washington, D.C. Area was organized. This still-vital group has been publishing their annual literary magazine, *Washington Munhak* (*Washington Literature*). Likewise, the Korean literary people in the New York area have been publishing *New York Munhak* (*New York Literature*) annually. At the same time, the Korean literary people of Atlanta, Chicago, and San Francisco have been producing similar magazines.

In 1996, the Korean Literary Society in Seoul hosted an international conference for overseas Korean literary people, and invited many prominent poets and writers from the United States, China, Japan, and several European nations. It was the first big conference of its kind. At the event, poet Cho Yoon-ho, based in Los Angeles, proposed a new, annual publication, *Haeoae*

Munhak (*Overseas Korean Literature*). In the first issue, he printed a story by Lee Hoi-sung and his dialogue with Yu Mi-ri, two prominent Korean writers who received the prestigious Akudagawa literary prize, in Japan. Cho attempted to network with overseas Korean poets and writers via his magazine.

In 1999, poet Ho-gill Kim, based in Los Angeles, organized *shijo* poets in the United States and Canada, while publishing an annual *shijo* magazine. Notably, *shijo* is not free verse; it has the traditional rhythm of poetry. In 2002, Los Angeles-based Soon-tae Song published *Munhak America* (*Literature in America*). This magazine is unique in that it bridges Korean literature to America and American literature to Korea. In the first issue, Robert Hass's selection of outstanding American poets and their poems included works by Elizabeth Bishop, Anthony Hecht, Linda Gregg, John Ashbery, Angela Ball, Anne Carson, and John Steinbeck, a dialogue with Sidney Sheldon, and a Rick Bass short story. It also introduced several famous Korean poems, essays, and short stories.

Forgotten and Ignored Literature

Despite the enduring efforts of Korean-American poets and writers, no one has paid much attention to them. I was greatly disappointed by the general overlook of Korean literature in the United States by some Korean scholars in America. It seemed that they did not want to know what was going on in Korean-American literature, since the indigenous literature of Korea was their only concern. So far as publications are concerned, though some university and academic presses have published East Asian Studies series containing Korean poetry and fiction, they have yet to consider publishing Korean-American literature.

Korean studies programs in American colleges and universities have established Korean literature classes, whereby the students are mostly second- and third-generation Koreans. They study Korean classics, such as *Chunhyangchun*, *Kuwoonmong*, and *Hong Gil-dong chun*, and contemporary literary works by Inhoon Choi, Suk-young Hwang, Moon-yul Lee, Sang-byung Chon and Un Ko, among others. But rarely have any Korean-American writings been included in these Korean literature programs.

Some Korean scholars think the creative writing of Korean-Americans do not belong in the framework of Korean literature because it does not have literary value. I disagree with them. Poet Nam-soo Park's poems, such as "Sea Gull," should be required reading. Already, Yearn Hong Choi's short story has been published as part of a major college textbook. Korean-American authors should not be ignored simply because of their geographical location. Perhaps Korean-Americans should receive increased funding to support their cause and gain more attention.

Resistance Poetry

A group of Korean poets in the United States published a couple of "resistance" poetry books against Korean military regimes in the 1970s and 1980s. Before and after General Chung-hee Park's assassination, a couple of Korean poets in America published political poems to denounce the military dictatorship. When General Doo-hwan Chun killed protestors in Kwangju in 1980, seven poets published *Bitu Bada* (*Sea of Rays*). The following year, they published *Ah, Kwangjuyo* and *Mudungsaniyo* (*Oh, Kwangju*; and *Mt. Mudung*) with Korean poets in Japan and *Bitsi Tanun Owol* (*May Burning in Rays*) in 1983, to dedicate their poems to those who fought against the military rule. Poet Ju Whang Kap led the seven poets. Poet Won Ko published *South Korean Poets of Resistance* (New York: Cross-Cultural Communications, 1980), with the poems of Kim Chi-ha, and other poets in Korea.

Literary Works in English

Won Ko also edited and translated the *Korean Poems in Contemporary Korean Poetry* (Iowa University press, 1970).

That was the first major introduction of Korean poems to the United States. He also published his own poems in English, *The Turn of Zero* (New York: Cross-Cultural Communication, 1974).

During his college days at Indiana University, Yearn Hong Choi published "America" and "To the Flowers of Indiana" in the *Indiana Daily*, and exhibited his poetry-art ensemble at Indiana University Union Building. The exhibit drew attention from the students, faculty, and local residents. AP and UPI covered the exhibit, given Choi's unique status as a Korean student on a major American campus.

In the 1970s, Choi's poems were discovered by Professor Paula De Paula of the University of Espirito Santo, Brazil, and translated into Portuguese and published in Brazil. De Paula and graduate students in his comparative literature class translated Choi's works. (Paula De Paula, *nacionalidade da lingua*, A TRIBUNA-VICTORIA, Subado 22 julho de 1978).

Choi published "A Poet" and "The Woods" in the *Wyoming* (1987, n.4) and "Arizona Desert" in *Mildred,* while a collection of his poems, *Autumn Vocabularies*, was produced at the Calcutta Writers Workshop, in 1990. Pulitzer-prize-winning poet Gwendolyn Brooks wrote a poem, "Yearn Hong Choi," for his first poetry book in English

In 1994, Choi read his poems in the United States' Library of Congress under the auspices of the Gertrude Clark Fund. This was a first for a Korean poet. The United States' Poet Laureate is based at the Library of Congress, while poetry reading remains a tradition in the library's poetry room. Choi has published several short stories, one of which was "Bloomington, Fall 1972," which was published in *Short Story International,* and a college textbook, *Intercultural Journeys through Reading and Writing*, edited by Marilyn Smith Layton (New York: HarperCollins, 1991). Later, a poetry book in English by a group of Korean-American poets was published in 1997, *Mother and Dove* (New York: Institute for Korean-American Culture). Julia Kyungja Im made the publication possible.

CONCLUSION

Haengja Kim, president of the Korean Poets and Writers Group in the Washington, D.C. area, created a poetry-art ensemble at a Georgetown art gallery in 1997 which was covered by the *Washington Post*. At the exhibit, poems in English were juxtaposed by corresponding paintings.

Summing Up

Sadly, for the most part, the literary work of second-wave immigrants has been circulated only among themselves. Meanwhile, readership of Korean literary works is extremely limited in the United States, while literary magazines in Korea do not allocate space for Korean-American poets and writers. Publication possibilities in prestigious Korean literary magazines are highly competitive among the nation's first-class poets and writers.

To get published in English in the U.S., the language barrier of writers and poets is the first hurdle, and the literary quality is the second hurdle, for them.

Overcoming the language barrier and improving the literary quality of their works are the tasks for Korean-American writers in the centennial year. Those who cannot overcome the language barrier are seeking their places inside Korea. Only very few will find successes in that endeavor. How to improve the literary quality depends upon their creative effort and labor. Talent should be the necessary ingredient, but writing and re-writing over and again will help. Stories should be appealing to the reader, but a certain kind of plotting suitable to a certain kind of story should be invented or discovered. That creates literary quality.

Some good, autobiographical novels by the first- and second-generation writers have been published in the United States. Non-fictional stories can appeal to the readership, but their literary quality has been questioned. Poetry is facing more serious problems, because rhythm does not reside in their poems and because English is not their native language. That has caused a serious problem, or barrier. Therefore, their poems are, at best, translated works from Korean into English.

The first generation Korean-American poets and writers have been ignored, forgotten, and neglected by the American and Korean literary magazines for a very long time. Unless they break through on the literary front in the United States, the situation will continue. First generation poets can rediscover Cathy Song's *Picture Bride* on the occasion of the centennial year, and first generation Korean writers can rediscover Amy Tan's *Joy Luck Club* as their writing model. This is the best advice that I can give to aspiring Korean-American poets and writers.

More titles from Homa & Sekey Books

Modern Fiction from Korea Series

Father and Son: A Novel by Han Sung-won
Translated by Yu Young-nan & Julie Pickering
ISBN: 1-931907-04-8, Paperback, $17.95

A Kiriyama Pacific Rim Noble Book winner

An age-old struggle between the generations of modern industrialization and the battle for democratic freedoms in Korea. The author explores the role of the intellectual in modern Korean society and the changing face of the Korean family.

Reflections on a Mask: Two Novellas by Ch'oe In-hun
Translated by Stephen Moore & Shi C. P. Moore
ISBN: 1-931907-05-6, Paperback, $16.95

Reflections on a Mask explores the disillusionment and search for identity of a young man in the post-Korean War era. *Christmas Carol* uses the themes of hope and salvation to examine relationships within a patriarchal Korean family.

Unspoken Voices: Selected Short Stories by Korean Women Writers
Compiled and Translated by Jin-Young Choi, Ph.D.
ISBN: 1-931907-06-4, Paperback, $16.95

Stories by twelve Korean women writers whose writings penetrate into the lives of Korean women from the early part of the 20th century to the present. Writers included are: Choi Junghee, Han Musook, Kang Shinjae, Park Kyongni, Lee Sukbong, Lee Jungho, Song Wonhee, Park Wansuh, Yoon Jungsun, Un Heekyong, Kong Jeeyoung and Han Kang.

The General's Beard: Two Novellas by Lee Oyoung
Translated by Brother Anthony
ISBN: 1-931907-07-2, Paperback, $14.95

In *The General's Beard*, a journalist tries to solve the mystery of a young photographer's death. In *Phantom Legs*, a young girl studying French literature meets a student wounded during demonstrations and begins an ambiguous relationship with him.

More titles from Homa & Sekey Books

Farmers: A Novel by Lee Mu-young
Translated by Yu Young-nan
ISBN: 1-931907-08-0, Paperback, $15.95

The novel is about Korea's Tonghak Uprising the 1894. A farmer-turned Tonghak leader who left the village several years ago in the wake of a severe flogging returns to his village to take revenge of his exploiters.

The Curse of Kim's Daughters: A Novel
By Park Kyong-ni. Translated by Choonwon Kang, et al.
ISBN: 1-931907-10-2, Paperback, $18.95, Available in October 2003

An engaging and heart-wrenching novel about the five daughters of a fishing fleet owner who are cursed by their fate. A fascinating story of Korean women masterfully told by one of the most important Korean women writers.

Modern Poetry from Korea Series

Selected Poems by Choi Seungho
Translated by Won-Chung Kim & James Han
ISBN: 1-931907-11-0, Paperback, $12.95, Available in October 2003

Selected poems by Choi Seungho, a poet with an unusual ability of observing the things around him and a critic of man's false desire in modern society.

Selected Poems by Moon Dok-su
Translated by Chang Soo Ko & Julie Pickering
ISBN: 1-931907-12-9, Paperback, $11.95, Available in October 2003

Selected poems by Moon Dok-su, a poet whose poetry is characterized by a spirit of experiment and exploration both in content and expression.

Selected Poems by Kim Seung-Hee
Translated by Kyung-nyun Kim Richards & Steffen F. Richards
ISBN: 1-931907-13-7, Paperback, $15.95, Available in October 2003

Selected poems by Kim Seung-Hee, a conceptually-oriented poet whose work is a blend of rigorous intellectualism and lyricism that borders on the sentimental.

More titles from Homa & Sekey Books

Flower Terror: Suffocating Stories of China by Pu Ning
ISBN 0-9665421-0-X, Fiction, Paperback, $13.95

"The stories in this work are well written." – Library Journal

Acclaimed Chinese writer eloquently describes the oppression of intellectuals in his country between 1950s and 1970s in these twelve autobiographical novellas and short stories. Many of the stories are so shocking and heart-wrenching that one cannot but feel suffocated.

The Peony Pavilion: A Novel by Xiaoping Yen, Ph.D.
ISBN 0-9665421-2-6, Fiction, Paperback, $16.95

"A window into the Chinese literary imagination." – Publishers Weekly

A sixteen-year-old girl visits a forbidden garden and falls in love with a young man she meets in a dream. She has an affair with her dream-lover and dies longing for him. After her death, her unflagging spirit continues to wait for her dream-lover. Does her lover really exist? Can a youthful love born of a garden dream ever blossom? The novel is based on a sixteenth-century Chinese opera written by Tang Xianzu, "the Shakespeare of China."

Butterfly Lovers: A Tale of the Chinese Romeo and Juliet
By Fan Dai, Ph.D., ISBN 0-9665421-4-2, Fiction, Paperback, $16.95

"An engaging, compelling, deeply moving, highly recommended and rewarding novel." – Midwest Books Review

A beautiful girl disguises herself as a man and lives under one roof with a young male scholar for three years without revealing her true identity. They become sworn brothers, soul mates and lovers. In a world in which marriage is determined by social status and arranged by parents, what is their inescapable fate?

The Dream of the Red Chamber: An Allegory of Love
By Jeannie Jinsheng Yi, Ph.D., ISBN: 0-9665421-7-7, Hardcover
Asian Studies/Literary Criticism, $49.95

Although dreams have been studied in great depth about this most influential classic Chinese fiction, the study of all the dreams as a sequence and in relation to their structural functions in the allegory is undertaken here for the first time.

More titles from Homa & Sekey Books

Always Bright: Paintings by American Chinese Artists 1970-1999
Edited by Xue Jian Xin et al.
ISBN 0-9665421-3-4, Art, Hardcover, $49.95

"An important, groundbreaking, seminal work." – Midwest Book Review

A selection of paintings by eighty acclaimed American Chinese artists in the late 20th century, *Always Bright* is the first of its kind in English publication. The album falls into three categories: oil painting, Chinese painting and other media painting. It also offers profiles of the artists and information on their professional accomplishment.

Always Bright, Vol. II: Paintings by Chinese American Artists
Edited by Eugene Wang, Ph.D., et al.
ISBN: 0-9665421-6-9, Art, Hardcover, $50.00

A sequel to the above, the book includes artworks of ninety-two artists in oil painting, Chinese painting, watercolor painting, and other media such as mixed media, acrylic, pastel, pen and pencil, etc. The book also provides information on the artists and their professional accomplishment. Artists included come from different backgrounds, use different media and belong to different schools. Some of them enjoy international fame while others are enterprising young men and women who are more impressionable to novelty and singularity.

Dai Yunhui's Sketches by Dai Yunhui
ISBN: 1-931907-00-5, Art, Paperback, $14.95

Over 50 sketches from an artist of attainment who is especially good at sketching stage and dynamic figures. His drawings not only accurately capture the dynamic movements of the performers, but also acutely catch the spirit of the stage artists.

Musical Qigong: Ancient Chinese Healing Art from a Modern Master
By Shen Wu, ISBN: 0-9665421-5-0, Health, Paperback, $14.95

Musical Qigong is a special healing energy therapy that combines two ancient Chinese traditions-healing music and Qigong. This guide contains two complete sets of exercises with photo illustrations and discusses how musical Qigong is related to the five elements in the ancient Chinese concept of the universe - metal, wood, water, fire, and earth.

More titles from Homa & Sekey Books

Ink Paintings by Gao Xingjian, the Nobel Prize Winner
ISBN: 1-931907-03-X, Hardcover, Art, $34.95

An extraordinary art book by the Nobel Prize Winner for Literature in 2000, this volume brings together over sixty ink paintings by Gao Xingjian that are characteristic of his philosophy and painting style. Gao believes that the world cannot be explained, and the images in his paintings reveal the black-and-white inner world that underlies the complexity of human existence. People admire his meditative images and evocative atmosphere by which Gao intends his viewers to visualize the human conditions in extremity.

Splendor of Tibet: The Potala Palace, Jewel of the Himalayas
By Phuntsok Namgyal
ISBN: 1-931907-02-1, Hardcover, Art/Architecture, $39.95

A magnificent and spectacular photographic book about the Potala Palace, the palace of the Dalai Lamas and the world's highest and largest castle palace. Over 150 rare and extraordinary color photographs of the Potala Palace are showcased in the book, including murals, thang-ka paintings, stupa-tombs of the Dalai Lamas, Buddhist statues and scriptures, porcelain vessels, enamel work, jade ware, brocade, Dalai Lamas' seals, and palace exteriors.

The Haier Way: The Making of a Chinese Business Leader and a Global Brand by Jeannie J. Yi, Ph.D. & Shawn X. Ye, MBA
ISBN: 1-931907-01-3, Hardcover, Business, $24.95

Haier is the largest consumer appliance maker in China. The book traces the appliance giant's path to success, from its early bleak years to its glamorous achievement when Haier was placed the 6th on *Forbes Global*'s worldwide household appliance manufacturer list in 2001. The book explains how Haier excelled in quality, service, technology innovation, a global vision and a management style that is a blend of Jack Welch of "GE" and Confucius of ancient China.

www.homabooks.com

ORDER INFORMATION
U.S.: $5.00 for the first item, $1.50 for each additional item. **Outside U.S.**: $10.00 for the first item, $5.00 for each additional item. All major credit cards accepted. You may also send a check or money order in U.S. fund (payable to Homa & Sekey Books) to: Orders Department, Homa & Sekey Books, 103-138 Veterans Plaza, Dumont, NJ 07628 U.S.A. Tel: 201-384-6692; Fax: 201-384-6055; Email: info@homabooks.com

Author Photos on the Back Jacket
Arranged from left to right
In the order as authors appear on the Table of Contents

ROW ONE
Nam Soo Park
Ko Won
Byong Hyon Kim
Yearn Hong Choi

ROW TWO
Haeng Ja Kim
Yong Pal Kim
Yoon Ho Cho
Jung Ja Choi
Sang Hee Kwak
Ho Gill Kim
Hye Young Hahn

ROW THREE
Soon Tae Song
Mee Soon Bae
Yong Chin Chong
Moon Hee Kim
William D. Chun

ROW FOUR
Sunghee Cho
Chungmi Kim
Chang Yun Lee
Samuel Changhyun Yim

ROW FIVE
Hye Shin Lim
Kwi Soon Kwon
Soon Paik
Ryang Suh
Young Kyo Kim
Duk Jae Shin

ROW SIX
Dae Wook Chang
Ke Hyang Lee
Wan Soo Byun
Jay Sang Rhee
Yong Ik Kim

ROW SEVEN
Sang Ok Song
Young K. Hahn
Elsie Hyeryung Kim
Seulhee Ahn

ROW EIGHT
Mia Yun
Kyung Sook Park